Praise for
Master Your Exit Plan

Creating a thriving business is a dream for entrepreneurs. Yet growing a business is all-consuming. While a lucrative exit is often back-of-mind, it is rarely planned or thoughtfully aligned with personal, financial or post-sale goals. In *Master Your Exit Plan*, Chris Vanderzyden provides a roadmap with easily understood steps and illustrative cases. This book is valuable to all business owners. As an entrepreneur myself, I wish I had these insights three businesses ago. This book is a must-read, whether you are a seasoned owner looking to sell a business or an entrepreneur just getting started.

— **James C. Fitchett,** Harvard University faculty

Entrepreneurship is the pillar that supports our communities. And every owner will inevitably exit their business. *Master Your Exit Plan* is a great educational tool that provides business owners with the necessary guidance to ensure a successful transition so their businesses and our communities will continue to thrive.

— **Steve Mariotti,** Founder, Network for Teaching Entrepreneurship

The second best way to "Master Your Exit Plan" is to have one! The best way is to have a master advisor to aid you in navigating the process. Chris Vanderzyden shows you how to navigate the obstacles and come out on top with any merger or acquisition!

— **Jeffrey W. Hayzlett,** Chairman and Founder, C-Suite Network

You spend your life building your business, and you only have one shot to sell it. Surround yourself with the right team and you will get the right results. *Master Your Exit Plan* is a must-read for any business owner, no matter what stage you are in. Chris Vanderzyden has tackled the issues all of us business owners face or will face and has laid out a roadmap for all to follow. Abraham Lincoln once stated, "A man who represents himself has a fool for a client." If you try to go it alone, well... Abe stated it well.

— **Mike Allen,** CEO, Flatirons Capital Advisors

Read this book to acquaint yourself with smart strategies that set you and your business up for the next chapter. Combining her seasoned expertise with the acumen of business planning advisors, Chris Vanderzyden, breaks down exit planning into thoughtful and manageable steps designed to optimize value—for you and your legacy. Clear. Instructive. Actionable.

— **Tracy Shaw,** Vice Chair,
SCORE Association Board of Directors

At Commonwealth Financial Group, we often encounter business owners who are considering the sale of their business but lack guidance. There is a lot to consider when selling your business and *Master Your Exit Plan* will provide you with practical advice and strategies so you can maximize your results upon exit. This is a must-read for all business owners.

— **Eric Spindt, CFP®,** President and Managing Partner,
Commonwealth Financial Group

As a business owner, I can attest to the fact that planning for my eventual exit seems overwhelming, and the exit strategy options are confusing. Chris has written a terrific guide with clear steps as to how to go through this process and strategies that will maximize the value of your business, while minimizing the stress on you. Read this book and be armed with the information you need for a successful transition to "what happens next."

— **Brian S. Crafts,** President, FMC Technologies

Master Your Exit Plan presents the often complex process of selling a business in a clear and concise manner. Chris Vanderzyden arms the reader with valuable information that will save sellers from making costly mistakes. The book is a must-read for every business owner, regardless of the stage of development of the business.

— **Pieter A. Weyts, JD, MBA**, Partner, NEXT Legal, PLLC

Author and Legacy Partners managing partner Chris Vanderzyden uses her decades of experience to enlighten readers on how to avoid many of the mistakes made when planning for and selling a business. *Master Your Exit Plan* will benefit all business owners—large or small. Read this book today, because your exit may be here before you know it.

— **Sharon Sayler, MBA, PCC**,
Founder, Competitive Edge Communications
and author of *What Your Body Says*
and *How to Master the Message*

Having a Master Exit Plan provided me with the information I needed to make the right decisions when I sold my business. Understanding the M&A process was critical when executing my Master Exit Plan and resulted in my receiving the best price and terms. If you want to be successful in selling your business, read this book. It will mean millions of dollars more in your pocket.

— **Paul Milano,** former Owner, Stellar Building Technologies

MASTER YOUR EXIT PLAN

Sell Your Business
Preserve Your Legacy

Other Books by Chris Vanderzyden
7 Steps to Entrepreneurial Victory

MASTER YOUR EXIT PLAN

Sell Your Business
Preserve Your Legacy

by
Chris Vanderzyden

Foreword by
John R. Hart, Vice Chairman
New York Private Bank & Trust

EMERALD LAKE
BOOKS
Sherman, Connecticut

Books published by Emerald Lake Books may be ordered through your favorite booksellers or by visiting emeraldlakebooks.com.

Library of Congress Cataloging-in-Publication Data

Names: Vanderzyden, Chris, 1964- author. | Hart, John R., writer of foreword.
Title: Master your exit plan : sell your business, preserve your legacy / by Chris Vanderzyden ; foreword by John R. Hart.
Description: [Sherman, Connecticut] : Emerald Lake Books, [2022] | Includes bibliographical references. | Summary: "Business owners don't have the knowledge necessary to sell their business and enter their post-ownership life with a full understanding of the financial and personal impact. The book provides a comprehensive strategy to successfully exit a business and presents the process to create a Master Exit Plan, which encompasses an owner's business, personal, and financial goals and maps the process to execute a successful sale"-- Provided by publisher.
Identifiers: LCCN 2022005780 (print) | LCCN 2022005781 (ebook) | ISBN 9781945847554 (paperback) | ISBN 9781945847578 (hardcover) | ISBN 9781945847561 (epub)
Subjects: LCSH: Sale of business enterprises--United States.
Classification: LCC HD1393.4.U6 V36 2022 (print) | LCC HD1393.4.U6 (ebook) | DDC 658.1/6--dc23/eng/20220324
LC record available at https://lccn.loc.gov/2022005780
LC ebook record available at https://lccn.loc.gov/2022005781

To my crew, Peter, Carling & Lillie,
who with great humor endured so many conversations
as I twisted and turned in writing this book. I drove
everyone crazy with a million pages strewn all over
the house as I put this puzzle together, but you were all
exceedingly patient with what seemed like
a never-ending project.

And to Tara, my amazing friend and publisher,
you are a gift to every writer. Only you could find
a spelling error in the Internal Revenue Code!

Contents

MASTER EXIT PLAN STEP I
Identify Your Business, Personal and Financial Objectives

Chapter 1. Where's Your Road to Wealth and Happiness? . . 1
A Master Exit Plan
How Matt strategically grew his business from $700,000 in revenue to $5 million in five years, culminating in a $40 million deal.

Chapter 2. Which Exit Door Will You Choose? 13
Explore the Six Primary Business Exit Strategies
  • Family Succession
  • Initial Public Offering
  • Employee Stock Ownership Plan or
    Management Buyout
  • Recapitalization
  • Liquidation
  • Outright Sale to a Third Party

Chapter 3. What Happens Next in Your Life? 29
Sam purchased his family business and sold it for big bucks, but then faltered. How he came to understand the importance of being emotionally prepared for his post-ownership life.

Design Your Post-Ownership Plan

Chapter 4. How Much Money Do You Need? 41
Create a Goal-Based Personal Financial Plan

Chapter 5. Who Can You Count On? .49
Identify Your Best-in-Class Team
- Exit Planning Advisor
- M&A Advisor
- Certified Public Accountant
- Wealth Manager
- Estate Planning Attorney
- M&A Attorney

MASTER EXIT PLAN STEP II:
Understand Your Business Value and Optimization Opportunities

Chapter 6. Will Your Business Attract a Buyer? 77
Assess the Eight Primary Transferable Value Drivers
- Strategic Plan
- Management Team and Human Capital
- Sales Process
- Marketing Plan
- Operations
- Finance
- Legal
- Contingency Plan

Chapter 7. What's Your Business Worth? 89
The Four Valuation Approaches
- The Income Approach
- The Market Approach
- The Asset Approach
- The Rule-of-Thumb Approach

MASTER EXIT PLAN STEP III:
Assess Your Business Risk

Chapter 8. How Risky Is Your Business? 105
The Five Big D's That Can Kill a Business

Buy-Sell Agreements

Nonqualified Deferred Compensation Plans

MASTER EXIT PLAN STEP IV:
Recognize When It's Time to Exit

Chapter 9. Do You Sell or Do You Grow? 123
The Opportunity Cost of Business Ownership

The Five Questions to Ask When Assessing Your Readiness

Chapter 10. What's Your Timing? 131
The Three Big C Economic Indicators

MASTER EXIT PLAN STEP V:
Understand the Steps to Sell Your Business

Chapter 11. Who Will Be Your Suitor? 143
*How Dawna chose a private equity group to buy 55 percent of
her company via a recapitalization structure for $45 million.*

Engage Your Deal Team

Create a Buyer Pool

- Financial Buyers
- Strategic Buyers
- Individual Investors

Chapter 12. How Will You Capture a Buyer's Attention? . . .155
Develop Compelling Marketing Collateral

- Confidential Business Profile
- Confidential Information Memorandum

Analyze Your Offers
- Indication of Interest
- Letter of Intent
- Management Meeting Preparation
- Corporate Culture Assessment

Chapter 13. Can You Get What You Want? 167
Negotiate Your Deal
- Price
- Structure
- Terms

Chapter 14. Will Due Diligence Kill You? 177
Due Diligence
The Close
- The Definitive Purchase Agreement
- Warranties, Representations and Indemnifications

John succeeded his father in the family business and after twenty-five years sold the business to a strategic buyer. The hardest part of his sale was breaking up with his employees.

- Company Integration and the Transition Period
- It's Not You; It's Me: How to Break up with Your Employees

MASTER EXIT PLAN STEP VI:
Protect Your Wealth, Family and Legacy

Chapter 15. Crossing the Finish Line 191
Invest Your Proceeds
Protect Your Wealth and Family

Acknowledgments 207

Glossary of Terms 211

Endnotes 221

Index 225

About the Contributors 235
- Jeffrey Carey, CFBS®, Vertex Planning Group,
  part of the Commonwealth Financial Group
- Michael Heberlein, CFP®, ChSNC®,
  Commonwealth Financial Group
- Jonathan Kim, JD, MBA,
  Jonathan B. Kim, PA/Legacy Partners, LLLP
- Tom Rogerson, President and CEO,
  GenLeg Company, Inc.
- Cathy Rogerson, Director, GenLeg Company, Inc.

About the Author 239

About Legacy Partners 241

Foreword

IN 1919, Morris Milstein founded the Circle Floor Company with nothing but his two hands. By 1960, his son, Paul Milstein, had led Circle Floor to success in the New York market, installing floors, walls and ceilings in many of New York's best known landmarks, including Rockefeller Center, the former World Trade Center and the new Madison Square Garden.

Paul Milstein then launched the family's first real estate development project in the 1950s. The Milstein vision was to invest in large scale developments that would serve to anchor and revive ailing neighborhoods. Paul, with his sons, Howard and Edward, developed a keen vision for identifying neighborhoods where they saw extraordinary potential long before most others. Today, the Milstein family owns both residential and commercial properties around the world.

In the 1980s, Howard Milstein further diversified the family's real estate portfolio and international business holdings into banking. The initiative culminated in 1986 with the purchase of Emigrant Savings Bank. Emigrant, a retail thrift bank founded in 1850 by the Irish Emigrant Society, was once the largest savings bank in the nation. Now, it is the country's largest privately owned, family-run bank. Expanding on this base, the Milstein family created New York Private Bank & Trust to serve the needs of other similarly successful families.

I have had the honor of working with the Milstein family as the president and CEO of Sarasota Private Trust Company and vice chairman of New York Private Bank & Trust Company. The Milsteins have exemplified the success of privately held business ownership and entrepreneurial stewardship for generations. We believe that in order to be successful in business, you begin by taking care of people. People are our priority, and we are committed to offering fully integrated investment advisory, trust, lending and other banking services to families.

We believe in entrepreneurship and honor the success of family businesses. We also recognize the unique needs of privately held business owners, as does Chris Vanderzyden and her team at Legacy Partners. They provide a critical service in guiding business owners through a comprehensive exit process that aligns an owner's business, financial and personal objectives. Their process reflects our philosophy to serve clients in a fully integrated fashion.

A business is often the most valuable asset for a family. But frequently there are gaps in the business owner's exit plan that could create a future financial loss if not corrected. We have collaborated with Legacy Partners as they analyze the risk within a business, and for the owners personally, to be sure the business and family are properly protected. Proactive planning ensures that a business is well positioned to attract an investor upon exit and that the owner can enjoy a successful sale that creates significant family wealth.

With high integrity, Legacy Partners seamlessly leads the business owner through their exit so we can then implement an investment strategy with full transparency, accountability and oversight to preserve the family legacy for generations to come.

Great family wealth is created through the endeavors of family businesses and, far too often, the wealth created by an entrepreneur is not fully realized due to a lack of planning for an owner's eventual exit. While successful entrepreneurs have an innate knack for launching and growing businesses, they often lack the knowledge of how to transition out of their role as business owner.

Exiting a business via a third-party sale requires a broad range of expertise, and the process is often perceived as complex and confusing. Chris, as an entrepreneur herself, has owned, operated and sold multiple businesses. Her decades of experience guiding entrepreneurs through the life cycles of business ownership has afforded her the ability to intimately understand the challenges owners face. With years of experience in the mergers and acquisitions industry, engaging with business owners in creating and executing their exit strategies, she is able to distill the complex process into an easily digestible plan of action.

Master Your Exit Plan is loaded with invaluable information to successfully exit your business and move onto the next stage of your life with financial security and confidence. The book presents case studies throughout, solidifying the information and serving as inspiration as you contemplate the sale of your business. Also included are expert contributors who present critical in-depth information on specific aspects of the sales process.

In our organization, we strive to educate our clients in many ways, but especially if they are business owners preparing for the sale of their company. I highly recommend *Master Your Exit Plan* as a resource for those clients and all business owners.

You've spent years creating great wealth in your business and now it's time for you to begin your transition from equity to liquidity. Read this book, then be prepared to take action and realize the financial security and legacy you've worked so hard to build.

— **John R. Hart,** Vice Chairman
New York Private Bank & Trust

Introduction

THE BUSINESS ENTERPRISE INSTITUTE estimates that approximately 81 percent of owners want to stop working in their businesses within the next ten years. Yet, 80 percent have no written exit plan.[1]

Most business owners are far too busy running their companies to plan for an exit they don't believe is imminent. Their focus is on immediate concerns, such as putting out fires to protect cash flow or tending to customers, vendors and employees. Moreover, many believe they'll never leave their business.

I've had owners tell me how much they love what they do and that they plan to die at their desk. "No exit plan needed!" Or one of my favorites, "I *am* the business. How can I exit myself?" This is the same rationale that underlies the often said, "If I never create a will, I'll never die." So, "If I don't intend to exit my business, why bother with an exit plan?"

Many owners wait to think about their exit until they either have an offer on the table or are being forced to exit their business by an unexpected event. You, however, may be the entrepreneur who has always dreamed of exiting your business by selling—a liquidity event that will allow you to retire and create enormous wealth for your family.

Or you may be in the position of having grown your business to the highest level possible with the resources available to you.

Now you're considering selling an equity stake to attract the capital and expertise needed to further scale your business to reach its true potential. And you need information on how to sell part of your business to recapitalize it, which generates a cash infusion to fuel future growth.

Or perhaps you are a budding entrepreneur who is just starting out. But you understand that preparing for your exit as early as possible will ensure that your business will be positioned to attract a buyer when the time is right. This requires understanding the information necessary to ensure that, as the company grows, your decisions will increase the value of your business.

As you think about exiting or trying to attract an investor, I know you're asking yourself, "how do I sell my business?" You may have received calls from buyer representatives or business brokers, or you may have received a direct call from a private equity group. You may feel uneasy and be thinking, "They just want to steal my company." And you may be right.

Financial buyers, such as a private equity group, buy multiple companies—their business is literally investing in businesses. Strategic buyers grow their companies through an acquisition strategy by absorbing businesses. These buyers are very sophisticated and have significant experience compared to you. Since you will most likely only sell a business or two in your lifetime and lack the in-depth experience and knowledge to navigate the process successfully, it is an unfair match, to say the least. This book will level the playing field for you. (Note that there is a glossary of common mergers and acquisitions terms for you to refer to if you need a translation for industry jargon.)

Then there is the financial aspect of selling your company. "Can I sell my business for enough money to go on to my next big plan?" You may also be concerned about what will happen to your employees, customers, brand and you! Your core identity may be completely wrapped up in the business, and you may be asking yourself, "If I sell my company, what would I do next? Will I regret selling?"

You probably have shoved these questions to the back burner many times. Yet your spouse or family may be nudging you, and you know, deep down, that time is ticking. You will have to exit at some point. But when is the right time to do it? "Is there a good time or a bad time to sell my business?"

It becomes confusing because there are so many unanswered questions.

- What is the value of my business, so I can be sure a buyer won't steal my company?
- Will the net proceeds be enough money to sustain my life at the same level I enjoy as a business owner?
- When should I sell?
- Who can help me reach buyers and guide me through the process?
- What will I do next?

Exiting your business via a third-party sale, the most common exit strategy, will require expertise in the mergers and acquisitions process, taxes, law, risk management, financial planning, and wealth management. It is a complex process, and if you feel confused as to how to sell your business and are not sure what to do, you are not alone.

Without knowing how to exit your business or who can help you navigate the process, you may choose to do nothing, which can be devastating to your future financial security. I've spent decades working with privately held business owners, and just when I think I've heard every sad exit story, another pops up.

A health crisis forced a business to close, and the owners did not have enough money to retire.

An entrepreneur launched a great business that had amazing potential but ran out of money before they could realize success.

The owner was relying on the sale of their business to fund the next chapter in their life, only to discover that their business wasn't positioned to attract a buyer. Instead, they became part of the 80 percent of businesses brought to market that never sell.

As an entrepreneur, I have launched, grown and sold multiple businesses. I know your pain. And as a CPA and a founding principal of Legacy Partners, an exit planning advisory firm specializing in mergers and acquisitions, I have spent years engaging with business owners, creating and guiding the execution of their exit strategies. I understand the confusion you feel and the need for clarity and guidance as you begin planning and executing the sale of your business.

The only way to exit your business from a position of control and clarity, resulting in a successful sale and a satisfying post-ownership life, is to have a Master Exit Plan (MEP) in place. A Master Exit Plan is a comprehensive step-by-step guide that will provide a business owner the information needed to take decisive action in preparation for the eventual sale of their business. It recognizes the inter-relationship of the owner's business, personal and financial planning. When executed successfully, your MEP will enable you to not only exit via a sale to a third party but also to transition into the post-ownership phase of your life with ease, confident your wealth will be protected for future generations.

A Master Exit Plan consist of six parts.

1. A business valuation.
2. Strategies to optimize the value of your business.
3. A personal financial plan.
4. Identification of the optimal exit strategy.
5. An estate plan review.
6. A post-ownership plan.

You can find information on these topics separately, but to exit successfully, a holistic approach that integrates your business, personal and financial planning is critical.

Your MEP will help you navigate the process of executing the sale of your business—resulting in the most important liquidity event in your journey as an entrepreneur.

I've written this book to empower you with information that will alleviate your confusion and serve as your guide as you work with a team that will create and implement your Master Exit Plan.

This book also presents the necessary steps to sell your business successfully. Information on public mergers and acquisitions deals is readily available, but the details of privately held businesses that sell are shrouded in confidentiality. So, how would an owner know how to sell their business?

Whether you are heading for the exit door today or searching for answers to help you down the road, this book will present the components of a Master Exit Plan and decode what often seems like dense or high-level mergers and acquisitions jargon.

Master Your Exit Plan will answer the following most pressing questions:

- What are the pros and cons of the available exit strategies?
- How do I determine if the sale of my business will produce enough liquidity for the next stage of my life?
- Who can help me plan and execute my exit?
- How is a business's value calculated?
- What qualities will make my business attractive to a buyer?
- Which type of buyer will meet my objectives?
- How do I prepare for my life post-ownership?

- When is the right time to sell my business?
- What is the process for selling my business?
- How do I protect my wealth post-sale and provide a legacy for my family?

This book is organized into six steps that, when combined, create your MEP.

1. **Master Exit Plan Step I:**
   Identify Your Business, Personal and Financial Objectives

   Assess the exit strategy options, create your post-ownership plan, establish your financial needs post-ownership, and identify the team you need to execute your plan.

2. **Master Exit Plan Step II:**
   Understand Your Business Value and Optimization Opportunities

   Analyze the eight primary value drivers and understand the business valuation methods.

3. **Master Exit Plan Step III:**
   Assess Your Business Risk

   Reduce risk in your business and increase enterprise value.

4. **Master Exit Plan Step IV:**
   Recognize When It's Time to Exit

   Discern when the timing is right and choose your targeted sale approach.

5. **Master Exit Plan Step V:**
   Understand the Steps to Sell Your Business

   Understand the mergers and acquisitions process to sell your business for the highest price and best terms.

6. **Master Exit Plan Step VI:**
   Protect Your Wealth, Family and Legacy
   Identify strategies to protect your family's security
   and future legacy.

Most owners of privately held businesses will want to exit by way of a sale to a third party, which is why this book is focused on that particular strategy. We will explore all exit strategies. However, I will not include extensive information in this book regarding the execution of a family succession, employee stock ownership plan, management buyout, or taking a company public, as each of these strategies has its own unique challenges.

I will present case studies from our practice at Legacy Partners. For a few of the studies, I've changed the names of the owners and their companies, as well as the buyers, to protect identities and respect confidentiality agreements. We'll start with Matt in our first chapter, who grew his business from $700,000 in revenue to $5 million in five years, then sold it for a whopping $40 million in total deal value. We'll also follow Dawna's story, who started her business from scratch to receiving a $45 million deal and retaining a minority equity position. You will also read case studies from owners who spent decades building their business and enjoyed a successful sale on a smaller scale.

I've also included contributions from experts who present critical legal information to consider when selling, strategies to reduce the risk in your business that will in turn increase its value, and advice on how to protect the wealth created from the sale of your business.

This book is your map to ensure you succeed in creating and executing a Master Exit Plan that will transition you from equity to liquidity, preserve your wealth, and provide a legacy for generations to come.

Enjoy!

Chris

MASTER EXIT PLAN PROCESS

 **Identify Your Business, Personal and Financial Objectives**

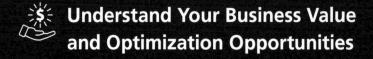 **Understand Your Business Value and Optimization Opportunities**

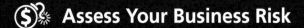 **Assess Your Business Risk**

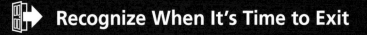 **Recognize When It's Time to Exit**

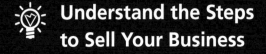 **Understand the Steps to Sell Your Business**

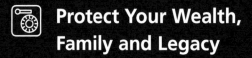 **Protect Your Wealth, Family and Legacy**

MERGERS & ACQUISITIONS PROCESS

 Identify Your Team

 Create the Buyer Pool

 Develop the Marketing Collateral

 Conduct the Limited Auction

 Analyze Offers

 Negotiate the Deal

 Sign Letter of Intent

 Perform Due Diligence

 Sign the Definitive Purchase Agreement

 **Close and Wire Funds**

MASTER EXIT PLAN
STEP I

*Identify Your Business, Personal
and Financial Objectives*

Chapter 1

Where's Your Road
to Wealth and Happiness?

HAVE YOU EVER WONDERED how a business owner becomes ultra-wealthy? We've all heard stories about the entrepreneur who uncovered the need for a product or service at just the right time. As someone who has owned many very hairy dogs, I have often wondered why I did not invent the Swiffer. Entrepreneurs like Gianfranco Zaccai, whose team did design the Swiffer, are very strategic. They carefully grow, launch and then sell their businesses for millions of dollars.

You may even have a friend or know someone in your industry who did just that. Is it luck? No. Luck is winning the lottery or being born into wealth. This is the result of careful planning.

At the core of every entrepreneur's success upon exiting their business is their ability to identify an opportunity that can be capitalized on and then to diligently plan and relentlessly execute their business strategy. Successful business owners go beyond the goal of just making money. They develop highly attractive businesses that can be scaled and sold at a premium, providing enormous financial security for their families.

The vast majority of businesses brought to market, however, do not sell, and the many reasons all point to one key issue—a lack of preparation.

While as an owner, you are very successful in running your business and may in fact be an expert in your industry, you most likely do not know how to prepare or execute the sale of your company. And you don't realize the importance of creating a comprehensive plan that addresses not only the exit strategy itself, but also your personal and financial needs. You see, the sale of your business is just one step in the process of creating great wealth.

At Legacy Partners, we have had many clients referred to us after they realized they were ill-prepared for their exit. Here are a few examples.

Jeff was approached by a private equity group that was swallowing up smaller players in his industry. They offered to buy his business for millions of dollars, and of course, were moving the deal along at lightning speed. The offer seemed great, and the proposal was more money than Jeff ever imagined filling his bank account! What troubled Jeff was that he had no idea what his business was worth. "Was this a good offer or were they attempting to steal my lifeblood from me?" he wondered. "What process should I be following? And after I do sell, then what?"

Jane inherited her business, a multi-generational company that had grown through good and bad economic cycles. They were able to continue innovating to keep the business relevant and competitors at bay. When it came time for Jane to retire, she struggled with the question, "Who will take the reins?" Her son had worked in the business for years, but Jane didn't think he had the necessary skills or drive to keep the momentum going. There also were the other kids in the family to consider. "How do I keep everyone happy?" Jane asked. "And how does the wealth accumulated in the business get distributed equally?" Her concern was, "If a family succession isn't in the cards, then how do I sell it and satisfy everyone?"

Frank was blindsided by a divorce. The business was a marital asset that needed to be divided equally, and if he wanted to maintain ownership and control, he'd have to buy out his wife's share. Regrettably, Frank didn't have the capital to do that. Does he take on debt to acquire her share of the business as part of the divorce, or is it better to sell? He wasn't sure if he wanted to let go of the business. Yes, he was close to retirement, but it was his baby! "Where will I find a buyer and how will I know if the offer's fair?" he asked.

Emily is a young entrepreneur who is trying to make her mark in the world of technology. She has a good shot with her plan to combine artificial intelligence with a blockchain platform, but last year she almost ran out of capital and nearly tanked her business. She didn't understand how to create value in a meaningful way that would attract investors. If her business does survive, with no exit plan in place, Emily may have serious voids that will reduce the company's enterprise value and threaten her ability to attract capital to fuel growth and exit the business successfully. Scared and unprepared, she asked, "How can I continue to fund my business?"

These experiences could have been avoided if the owner had a comprehensive strategic exit plan in place before these triggering events.

Business owners who succeed in realizing a liquidity event that results in enormous wealth start by creating a comprehensive Master Exit Plan (MEP) and then executing it flawlessly.

A Master Exit Plan

A Master Exit Plan is a roadmap that provides a business owner with the critical information needed to take decisive action in preparation for the sale of their business. It recognizes the interrelationship of the owner's business, personal and financial planning.

The following case study illustrates how one owner developed and executed his Master Exit Plan. The result was a successful sale that created enormous financial security for his family.

> **Matt** was an owner who strategically planned for his exit and sold his business. He'd spent decades in the insurance industry working for some of the largest firms, such as Lloyd's of London. But he wanted more than the corporate world could offer. He knew that running his own business could provide the security he wanted for himself and his family. His plan was to acquire a firm, build it up, and then exit by selling to a third party.
>
> Matt understood that a business is an asset through which he could receive a return on investment (ROI) if he properly built its transferable value, which, quite simply, is the value of a business without the owner in it.
>
> After working for a large brokerage firm, Matt moved to a regional firm to run their risk management division as an equity partner with the intent of eventually buying 100 percent of the shares. But sometimes events beyond one's control sideline the best of intentions. In this case, it was the global financial crisis of 2007–2008, which had an enormous impact on the financial industry.
>
> The firm suffered a financial blow, and the owners were unable to sell the company to Matt—or to any other buyer, for that matter. (There are many obstacles, some controllable and some not, that can prevent an owner from successfully selling their business. This is why having

a Master Exit Plan that creates contingency plans to contend with risks is so important to the success of your exit.)

Undeterred, Matt searched for another business to buy. His time in the corporate insurance world gave him expertise in a niche area of risk management using alternative funding mechanisms. He knew that his unique knowledge, if leveraged correctly, would position his business to be attractive to the larger players in his industry. Unlike most entrepreneurs, he was proactive and planned his exit strategy well before he chose to execute it.

Matt identified a dormant company to acquire. It was owned by an individual he'd known in the industry for years. The majority of assets had been previously sold off. So, what did Matt see in this comatose company? As he put it, "The business was established twenty-five years ago and had great name recognition, which gave the firm immediate longevity and avoided classification as a start-up—a potential cause for concern to new clients."

To get started, he bought the shell corporation for the brand. Intangible assets matter, and we'll talk about the value of your intangible assets, such as your brand, customer relationships, and employees, in "Chapter 7: What's Your Business Worth?" on page 89.

Matt bought out his minority equity position in the regional firm that was his original target. Then he brought twenty of his previous clients into the new company, and with three employees, started his business's upward trajectory.

His focus was solely on serving the company's niche expertise. As a result, the annual revenue exploded from $700,000 to $5 million in less than five years. By any standard, his results were impressive. But in the beginning, there were many sleepless nights, as every entrepreneur is familiar with.

Matt recognized that time was his most valuable asset, and in order to maximize his revenue per hour, he needed large, sophisticated clients who understood the value proposition his business offered.

As a first step, he leased office space in one of the most coveted buildings in Boston. With only three employees, 2,000 square feet of space was more than sufficient. But Matt wanted the corner office overlooking the city of Boston so he could impress his new clients. This is sometimes dubbed as "Fake it until you make it." But in reality, it's a solid strategy. He knew he needed to think big to compete with his competitors and stand out in a crowded field. So with a five-year lease for 6,500 square feet that had twelve offices, sixteen cubicles, and a $1.5 million personal guarantee, he went big!

The move was a stretch, but as Matt explained, "I wanted to play in the big leagues." And play he did. He signed the lease and built out every office and cubicle, posting phantom names of future employees on the doors to suggest greater depth and strength.

The lease was just one of several risky bets. Matt took no salary for the first year, and the sales cycle was long. It took at least twelve months to gain each new client. He was chasing high-premium clients and the hard work and patience paid off. His company was cited, year-over-year, as one of the top twenty-five largest and fastest-growing private companies in Massachusetts by the Boston Business Journal, and after five years, he was named one of the top twenty-five largest insurance brokers in the state.

That type of growth always gets noticed, and Matt began receiving calls from major firms that were in acquisition mode to support their own goals.

At this point, Matt stepped back and revisited his goal of creating real wealth for his family by exiting via a sale to a third party. As a risk management professional, he realized that he'd created a great company that was the largest asset in his family's portfolio. Uncomfortable with too many eggs in one basket—a common problem for privately held business owners whose largest asset is enormously illiquid—he was motivated to execute his strategy to sell and diversify his family's wealth. He understood, as he put it, "If I get hit by a bus tomorrow, the majority of the expertise is with me. So, what happens to my clients, my employees, my family?"

Matt also recognized that the timing was right in his industry. Selling prices, or "multiples of EBITDA" (earnings before interest, taxes, depreciation and amortization), were trending upward. The company had also grown so fast, they were having a hard time identifying qualified talent to support future growth. All indicators were pointing toward taking the company to market.

Often, a business owner will have a particular number in mind when it comes to the sale of their company. Whether it's a good or bad number is a different story.

Matt's financial goal was to sell his company for at least $10 million net after taxes and fees. He wasn't ready to retire, so his exit strategy was further refined to sell the company to a buyer who would provide more resources to fuel growth while allowing him to remain in the business. Matt's ability to maintain autonomy was also a critical factor in deciding which buyer from his auction would fulfill his goals.

He ended up selling the company to a large strategic buyer for $25 million cash; a three-year, $400,000 annual employment agreement with an earn-out bonus tied to growth; and 10 percent in stock, which translated to an EBITDA multiple of approximately 12x. He's currently on target to drive his total deal value after his three-year contract to over $40 million, which will result in a multiple of over 16x final EBITDA, not including any external investment gains on the sale proceeds.

Matt's exit strategy produced exactly what he wanted upon execution. Was it luck? No.

The key to Matt's success was that he had a strong business plan to support building a company with transferable value and a corresponding comprehensive MEP that identified his business, personal and financial objectives. His MEP provided guidance as he executed his plan.

- **Business:** Create enormous transferable value by leveraging his unique expertise, then sell to a large strategic buyer with capital to purchase the business at a premium.
- **Personal:** Exit the business while maintaining a position to contribute to the buyer's organization and participate in future growth while protecting his employees and clients.
- **Financial:** Diversify his family's wealth with a minimum of $10 million net after taxes and fees and protect the liquidity for the next generation and beyond.

As a result of his planning, Matt created a well-positioned company that could be sold successfully. The total time from business launch to exit was six years—much faster than he originally expected—but when the time is right, you go. Being prepared enabled Matt to realize a liquidity event that surpassed his expectations, and you can do this too.

I'm going to dive much deeper into Matt's deal throughout this book. We'll explore his preparation, market timing, buyer pool and every step of the sales process so you will understand the necessary considerations in the development and execution of your Master Exit Plan.

Business owners who identify their exit strategy and create a supporting plan at the beginning of their journey as an entrepreneur substantially increase their chances of reaching their exit goals. A proactive strategy guides all decisions as the owner scales the business, making the enterprise more attractive to their target buyers.

If you haven't created a Master Exit Plan, the sooner you take action, the quicker you can fix any issues that may prevent your business from being marketable.

Changes sometimes need to be made several years in advance. For example, developing predictable cash flow supported by a diverse customer base doesn't happen overnight. And if you have an underdeveloped management team (one of the most common flaws of a middle-market privately held business), it will take time to make the necessary adjustments.

As a business owner prepares to exit, there are three universal questions that every owner considers.

1. Who do I transfer the business to?
2. What happens next in my life?
3. How much money do I need to realize my goals?

A Master Exit Plan answers these questions, and it begins with identifying the owner's objectives.

Business Objectives

You've run your business for years. To what end? Most entrepreneurs agree the goal when they started their business was to create wealth and security for their family. How and when you choose to exit will ultimately determine the level of financial security you will create upon your liquidity event.

The key to identifying your business exit goal is to have a clear understanding of what your vision for the business is without you in it.

- Who will run it?
- What's the growth potential for your business?
- Who would be the right investor to continue growing the company?
- When do you want to exit?
- Is your business positioned to attract an investor?

Identifying what's meaningful to you and having a clear vision of the company's future will drive your decision as to which exit strategy will align with your business objectives. We'll explore the exit strategy options in the next chapter.

Personal Objectives

What are your aspirations when you are no longer a business owner? This isn't a question to be taken lightly. Selling a business is emotional for most owners. Many have stumbled post-sale as they realize how tightly their identity was bound to their company. With no office to go to, no meetings, and no direct reports, some former business owners find themselves sailing choppy waters in a rudderless boat with a bruised ego.

But, upon exit, the world is your oyster. You have the time and freedom to excel in other areas of your life. So how will you create new meaning in your life post-exit? It's important to be running toward something and not away from your business.

We'll get into post-ownership planning in Chapter 3.

Financial Objectives

If you're depending on extracting the wealth you created in your business to fund the next stage of your life, it's imperative that you understand not only what your next chapter looks like, but also what it will cost. Whether your goal is to fund your retirement, start another business, contribute to your community, or something else, you have to put a price tag on it.

We'll dive deeper into personal financial planning in Chapter 4.

Establishing specific objectives and goals is the foundation on which you'll create a Master Exit Plan that will ensure that you are not only financially secure post-exit, but happy. All the money in the world is meaningless if you are miserable after the sale. Each set of goals must be based on facts—not assumptions, guesses or hopes.

Antoine de Saint-Exupéry is credited with having said, "A goal without a plan is just a wish." However, whenever I quote Saint-Exupéry, I always add, "and hope is never a strategy."

By identifying your exit goals and creating a Master Exit Plan as early as possible, you'll dramatically increase your chances for a successful transition that provides wealth and a fulfilling post-ownership phase in your life. Let's begin by exploring which exit strategy is right for you.

TAKE ACTION

- Commit to creating your MEP by a specific date.
- Consider who could continue to grow the business after you exit.
- Contemplate your life vision for after your exit.

Chapter 2

Which Exit Door Will You Choose?

CREATING A MASTER EXIT PLAN begins with understanding your expectations for the business. Are you building a lifestyle business meant to generate a nice existence and cash to support your family? Has the company been in the family for generations and the expectation is that it will be passed on to the next generation? Are you building a rock star business that has a growth trajectory shooting to the stars, where you hope to take it public and become the next Amazon or Apple?

Perhaps you have key employees who would like to share in the ownership of the company you've built. Maybe you've imagined selling the business to a third party and getting a big payout. Or, you've had a lot of fun with the business, taking out some cash, and now you choose to close it.

Your business goals can become your destiny, with a plan to see it through.

According to the Exit Planning Institute, 67 percent of business owners in the United States do not know or understand their liquidity options.[2]

Explore the Primary Means to Exit a Business

There are six primary exit strategies.

1. Family succession
2. Initial public offering
3. Employee stock ownership plan or a management buyout
4. Recapitalization
5. Liquidation
6. Outright sale to a third party

We're going to explore each of these, along with their related pros and cons, in the rest of this chapter.

Family Succession

Transferring a business from one generation to the next sounds simple. Easy, just get Jim or Susie into the business, train them, and then slip out the back door. Right? Wrong! No other exit strategy brings out higher emotions than a family succession. And really... Think about it. Is your family sane?

My husband, Peter, had a family succession consulting company for years. He and his partners wisely sublet space in their building to a family psychologist. He'd joke that a family beginning an exit plan would come into his office and would immediately be sent down to the psychologist. When the psychologist gave the okay and emotions were settled, they were then welcomed back into his office. Only then could they begin the exit plan for a family succession.

Family Succession Pros

- You're keeping the asset in the family, and a family member is more apt to keep the business running just as you like it. This strategy can ensure a high level of privacy.

- It fulfills any promised family legacy. If the business has been in the family for multiple generations, there's an implied expectation that the next generation will be handed the golden egg.
- The transition can be quicker and less expensive. Due diligence will most likely be shorter since you don't have to deal with a pesky outside buyer.

Family Succession Cons

There often is a "family discount" involved in a family succession, making this strategy not as financially rewarding as other options. You'll also have to substantiate the discount to the IRS. In addition, the failure rate of a family succession is dismal.

According to a PricewaterhouseCoopers survey, 70 percent of family businesses fail to transition successfully from the first to the second generation and only 5 percent survive to a fourth generation.[3]

- The first generation makes it.
- The second, enjoys it.
- The third, destroys it.
- The fourth, buries it.

Schwinn was the top bicycle brand for generations. If you were born before 1980, no doubt you learned to ride on one. In 1979, the company was handed to the fourth generation.

Set in his ways, Edward Schwinn, great-grandson of Schwinn's founder Ignaz Schwinn, turned a blind eye to innovation in the industry. He ran the company in the same outdated facility in Chicago. Only Schwinn male family members were allowed to lead the company. In addition to being leadership deficient, they were also capital-constrained, and Edward refused outside financing. He ran the company just as it had always been run, with no female leaders and believing that all debt is dangerous.

Dismal marketing allowed other brands to steal market share, and the fourth generation led the company into bankruptcy with one bad decision after another, burying the family legacy.

There are many reasons for the failure of a family succession strategy.

- There may be a lack of passion in the next generation, inadequate preparation, or a misalignment of skill sets. Or perhaps the previous generation just can't let go, and they muck it up for the heir apparent. Families tend to be rooted in tradition and often subscribe to the philosophy that what worked for past generations will continue to work today. This belief often proves to be a nail in the business's coffin.

- You may find yourself emotionally and financially tied to the business forever. The next generation generally doesn't have the money to buy the parents out, so most often there will be a long-term promissory note as payment. The founding generation's salary now becomes the payout. Get ready for Thanksgiving dinners to include questions about the business, and if times get tough, your note may be the last to get paid. Your financial security is now chained to the company you thought you'd left, and if the next generation fails, your retirement—and their inheritance—may go with it.

- It may not be possible to create an equal distribution of assets between children who work in the business and those who do not. Passing the business down is an emotional decision for parents, and of course, every parent believes they treat and love each child equally. The catch is that what's equal is subjective in the eyes of the children, and this often causes the next generation to go to war, thus killing the business and fracturing the family.

Of course, there have been many successful family transitions. Levi Strauss & Co. has been handed down through multiple generations in the Haas family. Zildjian, the percussion instrument manufacturer, is the oldest privately held business. Started by an alchemist in 1623, it is now run by the fifteenth generation of the family who are in the fourth century of the business!

Why are they successful? Because the shift began many years before the actual transition occurred. Rigorous planning ensured that the next generation was prepared to run the business and the tax implications were recognized and mitigated.

I've spoken with many nervous parents who are unsure whether the next generation is capable of running their business. Often, the concern is centered on the son or daughter having the work ethic required to manage and grow the operation. They may even suspect that perhaps the next generation is more interested in the financial rewards and lifestyle the business offers rather than the business itself.

"How do I know they really want the company?" these parents ask.

The number one reason the next generation fails is a lack of passion. It isn't their baby. So, the first question that needs to be answered is, "Is the next generation passionate enough about the company that they will have the fortitude to make it through the bad times?"

The involvement of the next generation is very different today than it was in the past. It used to be that the family business involved relatives of all ages daily. Today, the next generation is engaged in outside pursuits; playing sports or whatever activity holds their interest. When asked about taking over the enterprise, the next generation may shun the very idea. Often, the perception is that the parents wasted their lives working hard building something the kids want no part of.

If your exit strategy is succession within the family, ask yourself the following pivotal questions:

1. Is the next generation passionate about the business, and is it their dream or yours?
2. Do they have the skills to run and grow the business successfully?
3. Are you financially and emotionally prepared to let go of the business?
4. Do you have an actionable transition plan in place that will ensure success for both generations?

Initial Public Offering

You've worked hard building your business and capitalized it with a bootstrap financial strategy. Perhaps you relied on savings, credit cards, friends, family and any other way you could dig up a penny. The business has made it through the dangerous early stages and is officially off the ground. Your operation has grown with the resources available, and research shows that there is indeed further growth potential, if only there was capital available to fuel the expansion. This is where initial public offerings (IPOs) come into play.

As mentioned earlier, Levi Strauss was a privately held business handed down to multiple generations until the family could no longer fund additional growth. They decided to take the company public in 1971 to raise much-needed capital to grow to the next level of complexity. The descendants then took it private again in 1985 and public a second time in 2019.

Going public gets press and is exciting, but pay attention to the pros and cons.

IPO Pros

- The sky's the limit, or at least, the growth potential can be realized to the extent that capital is raised.
- It's really cool to say your business went public. It's a big sexy feather in the cap of an entrepreneur.
- Success breeds success. There's only one coming out party, and if you're successful, it just gets easier to raise more capital in the future.

IPO Cons

- It's expensive, with underwriting being the biggest expense. Then there are other headaches like the legal aspects, accounting, registering with the US Securities and Exchange Commission (SEC), and filing with the Financial Industry Regulatory Authority (FINRA).
- Now you've got demanding shareholders, and perhaps an even more demanding board of directors.
- Welcome to the world of extensive reporting to the SEC and adhering to the Sarbanes-Oxley (SOX) Act.

If the vision for your business includes a BHAG (big hairy audacious goal) to exit via an IPO, how do you know it will be successful?

You don't. But you may want to consider the following:

1. Are you ready to give up 100 percent equity?
2. Do you have a verified and compelling case to go public?

3. Is the idea of having shareholders, board members, and extensive oversight appealing?
4. Do you have the right team in place for the required rigorous financial reporting?

Employee Stock Ownership Plan or Management Buyout

You've grown your business and feel that your employees and managers have been critical to your success. Now, you'd like to reward them by selling the business, either directly to key management, to an employee group, or to all employees through the establishment of an employee stock ownership plan (ESOP).

ESOPs are essentially tax-qualified defined contribution retirement plans, or more simply put, they're trusts that buy, hold and sell a company's stock for the benefit of its employees.

A management buyout (MBO), meanwhile, is a sale to key managers.

ESOP or MBO Pros

- If you believe your employees and management team have the right skill set to lead and grow the business without you, this can be a viable transition. It's been proven that employee ownership is a strong motivator that drives success. Also, these two exit strategies allow you to carry on the brand identity and, traditionally, your business legacy will be fulfilled.
- The tax advantages of an ESOP can be significant to those companies that are structured as a C-Corp.
- An MBO transition tends to be relatively smooth and private.
- If the M&A market is in a buyer's cycle, meaning there is a high supply of businesses and low

demand, setting the selling price using an independent valuation will most likely outperform an open market price.

ESOP or MBO Cons

- Selling to employees or the management team typically will add debt to the balance sheet as they borrow money to fund the ESOP or leverage the MBO. Also, when an employee departs, the ESOP is required to buy back the shares at the current enterprise value. Looking forward, forced stock buybacks may place stress on ESOPs as more baby boomer employees retire.

- Setting up an ESOP is expensive. Then, once it's established, it requires ongoing financial support to administer the plan and adhere to the rigorous reporting required under the SOX and ERISA regulations. The latter of these involves corporate oversight from the Department of Labor, IRS and SEC.

- If the M&A market is in a seller's cycle, meaning there is a low supply of businesses and high demand, the valuation used for the ESOP to set the price could underperform the open market. As a result, if you sold on the open market, you would most likely garner a higher price from a strategic buyer.

There are many successful transitions via an ESOP or MBO. However, there have been many that have gone south. Sierra Aluminum is an example of an ESOP that went off the rails when the employees complained to the Department of Labor that they'd been saddled with too much debt. They used the "Doctrine of Fraudulent Conveyance" to sue the owner. The assumptions used by GreatBanc for the valuation of their ESOP were questioned, and the Department of Labor sided with the employees. This resulted in the ESOP being unwound, forcing the owners back into the business.

Here are a few thoughts when considering a sale to employees.

1. Are you confident that your leadership team has the skills to grow the business and ensure continued success?
2. Have you considered the tax implications and extensive reporting requirements?
3. Are you prepared to give up some or all control of the company?

Recapitalization

A recapitalization is a unique, third-party sale structure that affords an owner a liquidity event while retaining an equity position. Perhaps you've built your business to the highest level you can based on your capital availability and expertise, but you believe the business has potential to grow exponentially if you had additional resources.

A recapitalization, in its most simplistic form, is a partial sale. A private equity group, private investment group, or family office group buys your business, and at close, you buy back an equity position.

The buyer then becomes a financial investor in your business, bringing both capital and expertise to the table. For example, a company in California had saturated their geographic market but knew there was tremendous growth opportunity through a franchise model. Not having the expertise or capital, they sold an equity stake to a PEG to help them realize their growth potential.

Recapitalization Pros

- A recapitalization allows a business owner to grow with a financial partner who brings both business acumen and capital to the table. The goal of most PEGs is to double the value of the business within two to three years, triple in three to five years, and quintuple in seven to ten years. Ultimately, a financial investor's exit strategy will be to sell the business to a larger group or take it public, providing the business owner with a second bite of the apple.

- A partial sale gives the owner liquidity while maintaining an equity position. It also reduces the owner's risk since they no longer carry 100 percent of the burden.

- If one partner wants to leave the business and the other wants to stay, a partial sale is a strategy that will satisfy both goals. It's also a successful strategy executed in conjunction with a family succession plan.

Recapitalization Cons

- You no longer have 100 percent control over the business.

- Financial investors like to know what's going on with the business they invest in, so expect lots of reporting to your new partner.

- There may be expected financial distributions to the investor regardless of the business's performance.

Is a recapitalization right for you? It's hard to say for certain. But here are a few questions to ask yourself as you decide.

1. Is your main objective to stay for a time to help grow the company?
2. Do you need capital and expertise to fuel future growth?
3. Are you prepared to give up a portion of equity and control?
4. Do you understand the financial and risk implications both personally and for the business?

23

Liquidation

Whether purposefully or by force, many privately held businesses have met their demise by closing the company. At times, liquidation may be exactly what the business owner intended all along, though.

During my time lecturing at Harvard, two students created a business to teach leadership training on a sailboat. Cambridge, Massachusetts, is on the Charles River, where crew and sailing are much loved sports. This business model had inherent scalability and cash flow issues related to its seasonal nature. The capital to scale a leadership training program on a sailboat was massive, and eventually, the Northeast freezes over every year, drying up revenue. The students, however, loved to sail, and this passion-based business was relegated to a lifestyle business. Their exit strategy was to have a lot of fun while running the company, bleed it dry, and then close it.

Liquidation Pros

- It's relatively quick and easy to do.
- The timing of the transition is whenever it feels right to you.
- There's no future risk from any contingent liabilities.

Liquidation Cons

- There's no big payoff for building the business.
- The legacy built with your business vanishes.
- Employees may be less than thrilled.

Is closing the doors your best option? Here are some questions to reflect on before deciding.

1. Are you comfortable with any value, including intangible assets, such as your customer list,

reputation and employees, vanishing in liquidation with no return on your investment?

2. Is your return-on-investment expectation simply the market value of your liquidated assets?
3. Will you be satisfied with the disappearance of your legacy?

Some owners may think that liquidating their business is the only option. Yet you'll want to look closely at the alternatives before settling on this choice.

I had a business owner come to me after a December speaking engagement to explain that, with his CPA's guidance, he had decided his exit plan was to close his doors effective December 31. He was a plumber and had built his business over forty-two years. He was "tired and ready to retire!" After all those years of effort put into building the business, I couldn't imagine that closing the doors was his best option, but I did understand his being tired.

I asked a few questions, such as who his customers were, to which he replied that he "serviced commercial buildings." Ah, not the run-of-the-mill home kitchen sink plumber, I thought.

So, I asked, "Do you have contracts with these commercial buildings?"

He responded, "Yes, we have some buildings we've been servicing for over twenty years."

Now I'm thinking about recurring revenue—buyers love future predictable cash flow supported by maintenance contracts.

So, I pushed on. "How many employees do you have, and approximately how much revenue are you generating annually?"

He replied, "About twenty-five employees on average, and we're a bit under three million in annual revenue."

"EBITDA?" I ask.

"About one million," he responded.

So, this owner has been in business for forty-two years servicing commercial buildings, has twenty-five employees, is generating $1 million in EBITDA, and he is going to close it? I understood he was tired, but he deserved to get more than book value for his business.

With the help of an experienced M&A team, he received a healthy return on investment by selling to a third party.

Outright Sale to a Third Party

External buyers are attracted to a business because they see value that can be capitalized on to create a return on their investment.

Outright Sale Pros

- A third-party sale through a controlled auction on the open market often results in a higher return on investment than other exit strategies.
- The deal can be structured to protect employees and typically may afford the seller the opportunity to remain active in the business.
- An outright sale takes away the risk of owning a business. Entrepreneurs are risk-tolerant, but as they become more successful and amass significant assets, they look toward reducing their risk by selling and diversifying their investments.

Outright Sale Cons

- A successful sale requires extensive planning and typically can take nine to fourteen months to complete.
- Market timing is an important aspect of selling your business successfully. If the timing is right, premium prices are paid. But if the M&A market cycle is down, businesses can sell for pennies on the dollar.

- After the sale closes, the business owner may be constrained from working in the industry because of a noncompete agreement.

Is an outright sale of your business the right exit strategy for you? Consider the following:

1. Is your business positioned to attract buyers?
2. Can you credibly document the growth potential of your business?
3. Do you have a post-ownership and financial plan in place ensuring you're emotionally and financially prepared to exit?

These considerations are the basis for creating a profitable exit strategy via a sale to a third party. The reasons selling a business makes sense are varied, and there's no wrong answer. Like my plumber friend, you simply could be tired or bored. I've also worked with thirty-year-old serial entrepreneurs who want to release capital from one business to invest in the next.

Remember, Matt's exit plan was to sell to a third party with the understanding that a large strategic buyer would deliver the highest return on investment. He was cognizant of building a business with transferable value and astute to market conditions. He was also able to time his exit when the multiples being paid in his industry were high. We'll discuss optimizing transferable value and market timing in detail later in this book.

The exit strategy identified to meet your business goals should be planned well in advance, so when it's time for your exit, you can do so successfully. The most common strategy is to sell the business to a third party, and we will focus on that in the coming chapters.

TAKE ACTION

- Analyze how mature your business is today and what the future growth potential is.
- Consider any existing internal constraints that may impede growth, such as leadership gaps or capital deficiencies.
- Assess which exit strategy could potentially meet your business objectives, based on the presented pros and cons.

Chapter 3

What Happens Next in Your Life?

IN ASSESSING WHEN TO EXIT, one of the most common questions is, "If I sell my business, will I have enough money to support the next phase in my life?" It's an important question, and the answer lies first in establishing your financial goals as part of your MEP. In other words, what's your vision financially for your future?

You can't assess your financial needs without first creating a post-ownership plan and understanding how much the next chapter in your life is going to cost. So, before we get into your financial goals, you'll need to gain some clarity on what your post-ownership life looks like. Then, you can put a price tag on it.

Establish Your Personal Goals

Identifying your professional and personal goals is the first step in creating a post-ownership plan, which is an integral part of your MEP. Most owners have never thought about the possibilities and certainly haven't planned for it.

We've had clients who've dug their heels in and insisted that they'll never leave their business. There are also plenty of owners who feel that their business is valuable, their market sector ripe with investors, and they're ready to sell and ride off into the sunset. But, we need to know what that "sunset" looks like.

Business owners are often slow to develop their exit plan. However, once they understand the risk of not planning their exit and that it won't be painful or complicated, they have some fun with it and start to dream about the possibilities for their life post-ownership.

Some want to retire, sit on a beach, go fishing, travel the world, or see the grandkids more.

Others may want to get back in the game and start a new business. Many are serial entrepreneurs who love innovation and want to go on to the next great challenge. Some qualify that statement by insisting the next business will be easier, simpler, less risky.

Very often I hear business owners say, "I want another business, but with no employees!" That always makes me laugh.

And many want to give back to their communities at a higher level.

Whatever your goal, it must be carefully planned so there are no regrets after you sell.

According to the Exit Planning Institute's Owner Readiness Survey, 75 percent of business owners experience "seller's remorse" one year after selling.[4]

It's hard to believe that a business owner who accomplished a liquidity event that brought them tremendous financial security and freedom would experience remorse. So, what fuels this regret?

- The owner questions if they actually received the highest price for their business. Without proper financial planning, they misunderstood the deal structure, terms and the tax impact. As a result, they were never clear about how selling their business would affect their financial future.

- In hindsight, the former owner now believes that the new owner wasn't the right choice culturally for the employees. They worry their customers will not be taken care of, that the business will decline, and that their legacy will be forever tarnished.

- No consideration was given to their post-ownership existence. As a result, the owner was emotionally unprepared to sell their business and move on to the next phase of their life.

The primary reason is that many owners experience an enormous loss of identity, diminished sense of passion and purpose, undermined social structure, and lack of direction.

Some business owners who ended up pining for their old business during their noncompete period reacted by launching unrelated new businesses in an effort to ease the regret, only to fail miserably and lose a great deal of the money they made selling their old business.

> **Sam,** the youngest child—and the only one of four children with an interest in the family business—decided to study finance in college before joining his father's company. After graduation, he took the highest paying job he could find in the financial services industry to learn the ropes, eventually landing on his father's doorstep.
>
> His introduction to running the family business was expedited by having to replace the controller immediately, who had suffered a sudden heart attack.
>
> "It was a bit of a trial-by-fire situation," Sam said.
>
> Still, he earned his wings quickly, preparing him for the multitude of challenges that he would encounter along the way as the business grew.

When he purchased the business from his father, it made him a third-generation owner. Typically, as previously mentioned, a family discount is given to the next generation. But in this case, while it appeared as if Sam paid the market price of $1.5 million, the terms afforded payment over fifteen years. In effect, this was the family discount that gave him the capital needed to execute his growth plan.

With fifteen employees, he set out to expand the business through an acquisition strategy. Over the course of nineteen years, Sam purchased thirteen companies and drove the business to seventy-five employees and $11.2 million in annual revenue.

Sam recognized that if he wanted to continue to cultivate the business by obtaining more sophisticated clients, he needed a larger brand behind him. Being acquired by a strategic buyer with a national reach would allow him to "swim upstream more effectively." So, having grown the company to its highest potential with the resources available to him, he decided to go to market.

His company sold for $36 million cash and a 10 percent stock option, which tripled in value thereafter, plus a three-year employment agreement with an earn-out that resulted in another $4.5 million bonus at the end of his contract.

While Sam did so many things right in strategically growing his business, understanding value, aligning himself with the right team to execute his transaction, and so on, he faltered post-ownership. His reaction after the sale was, "Wow! I made a lot of money. This is great!"

But shortly thereafter, he said, "It was emotionally awful." Sam was officially part of the 75 percent of owners who regret having sold their business.

Having lost his twenty-year identity and the community that he had relied on for so long as a business owner, Sam struggled with depression and admitted he was "completely unprepared emotionally for the transition."

Straining to create a new identity, Sam partnered with another owner who'd also recently sold his company and purchased a business that supplied corks to wineries. They imported corks from Portugal, branded them with the winery logo, and then sold them to customers. On the surface, it seemed to be a straightforward operation, but a critical error in due diligence ultimately caused the business to fail.

The cork supplier was providing verification of compliance for 2,4,6-Trichloroanisole (TCA) testing (for cork taint), which is a mold byproduct that causes an unpleasant aroma in wine. After receiving complaints from customers, Sam and his partner had an independent test for TCA performed that revealed their inventory contained high levels—effectively making it unsalvageable.

With no inventory, Sam and his partner resorted to buying TCA-compliant corks at full retail price to fulfill customer orders while searching for a new supplier. The loss was enormous.

Eventually, they identified a new supplier, but the cost of the new inventory was much higher and the price increase in a low-margin business forced them to close.

If Sam and his partner had commissioned industry-specific due diligence on the inventory, they would have saved themselves from making a poor investment. More importantly, if Sam had had a Master Exit Plan with a documented post-ownership plan in his back pocket, he would have been prepared for the next chapter in his life. It's unlikely then that he would have purchased a business he knew nothing about, in a knee-jerk fashion.

Sam recovered, no longer regretting selling, and after his noncompete period was over from the sale of his first business, he went on to buy another in the same industry.

When asked about his experience investing in another business soon after the successful sale of his first company, he advised, "Stick with what you know and be prepared emotionally for the sale of your business."

It's always better to be going toward a planned new phase in your life, rather than running aimlessly from the past.

Having a passion, purpose and vision that extends beyond business ownership ensures that the owner will have a sense of fulfillment in their life once the business sells. An entrepreneur never really retires. They re-launch their life, focusing on what's now meaningful to them and their family.

Regardless of your specific goals, if well-planned, you won't regret selling your business. But your plan must encapsulate the fulfillment of both your emotional and financial needs.

This is often referred to as the "soft stuff" in exit planning, and you may even be rolling your eyes at the very thought of focusing on yourself. However, if you don't pay attention to this part of the planning process, all the nitty-gritty legal, tax, financial and M&A information in this book won't mean a thing, because you won't be happy after you sell. Money doesn't matter if you're miserable.

We at Legacy Partners guide our clients through five exploratory exercises, well before selling a business, to create a meaningful post-ownership plan. That way, the seller can ride off into the sunset with no regrets.

1. Understanding yourself.
2. Exploring your dreams.
3. Designing your life.
4. Creating powerful goals.
5. Organizing your plan for success.

Understand Yourself

Throughout your ownership, you've focused solely on the business, and now we want you to shift and think only of yourself. I know it seems selfish having been focused on customers, suppliers and employees for so long. But after you sell, it's your time. And if you don't plan now, there's a good chance you'll join the club that regrets selling their business.

What makes a business owner wealthy? Happiness. It's ultimately not how many dollars are in the bank, but the fulfillment you derive from life.

The best example of happiness is when what you say, do and think are in harmony. It's astounding how many business owners have no idea what will make them happy. They've simply been on the ownership treadmill too long with very little time to focus on themselves. So, begin by uncovering the path to a productive and fulfilling life after you, the owner, have exited your business.

The process starts by understanding the values you want to bring to your life and work, as well as the personal needs that must be met if you're to lead a productive and fulfilling post-ownership life.

Explore Your Dreams

It's time to make a bucket list! Have some fun exploring your dreams. I love the saying "Go big or go home!"

Start by reflecting on all the dreams you've had about what the future might hold. Focus on these four facets of life.

1. What you'd like to *do*... such as self-development, artistic pursuits, or public service.
2. Who you'd like to *be*... such as a community leader, lecturer or mentor.
3. Places you'd like to *go*... be specific, not just "travel."
4. Things you'd like to *have*... such as a boat or plane.

Choose dreams to pursue in all areas of your life: career, relationships, artistic pursuits, health and fitness, education, personal development, and so on. Some dreams may be large, like starting another business. Others will be smaller, like spending four days in Rome.

Design Your Life

Since life is really about choices, not circumstances, you can now focus on your dreams and prioritize those that are the most important to you.

Your post-ownership life design will focus on three main drivers: intellectual, physical and social.

Intellectual

Identify what will continue to stimulate you. You've mentally engaged in building a business over many years. How will you fill the void and focus your attention on a new passion?

- Volunteer your professional skills to a nonprofit?
- Develop suppressed talents?
- Participate in a mentoring program?
- Audit college classes?

> Statistically, 48 percent of business owners have no post-ownership plans, 27 percent intend to buy or invest in another business, and 28 percent will engage in philanthropic activities.[5]

Physical

Where you live and how you maintain your physical and emotional health to ensure you can enjoy the next stage in your life is very important. What will you do physically and what activities will you engage in?

- Will you live in a tax-free state? The South of France?
- How will you maintain your health? Playing tennis, skiing, riding?
- Do you dream of visiting an ashram?
- Do you want to hike Machu Picchu?

Social

Our social network supports us through our greatest transitions, and exiting a business is a landmark change. Often our relationships as an owner center on people we do business with.

Upon exit, a business owner may feel their social circle has shrunk. So in preparation, it's important to plan how you'll sustain social connectivity post-ownership. Sam, who regretted selling his business, blamed the loss of his social circle as a main contributor that fueled his regret.

What's your social plan?

- Reinvigorate relationships that may have faltered as you focused on running your business?
- Expand your social network outside of business through volunteering?

- Focus on family relationships?
- Join a civic organization, spiritual center or club?

Many studies support the importance of social connection on our happiness and health.

> Harvard Health Publishing cited one study that found a lack of strong relationships increased the risk of premature death from all causes by 50 percent.[6]

Create Powerful Goals

Now that you understand your values, have identified your needs and dreams, and designed your life intellectually, physically and socially, it's time to create compelling goals that make that future vision a reality.

An excellent technique for goal setting is to define "SMART" goals. These are:

- Specific
- Measurable
- Achievable
- Relevant
- Time-bound

By setting goals, you'll be able to map your progress along the route, keeping the focus on your ultimate destination. What's more, you can quickly distinguish between activities that contribute to the achievement of your dreams and the distractions that get in the way.

Organize Your Plan for Success

By this stage, you've converted your dreams into positive, attractive goals. Where these are particularly large, you have milestone goals that will help you measure progress along the way.

A common stumbling block to goal achievement is scheduling the time to focus on them. It's important to create an integrated organizational system that draws on your years of experience running and operating a business.

This final step is crucial for the achievement of your post-ownership goals and the enjoyment of the next stage in your life. As a business owner, you know how to do this since this step draws on years of your business acumen.

———————————

Now that you've established your personal goals post-exit, the next step is to put a price tag on it.

TAKE ACTION
- Identify what will continue to stimulate you intellectually after you are no longer running the business.
- Determine what you will do to maintain your physical and emotional health.
- Create a plan to develop a social network that is not focused on your business contacts.
- Establish specific goals to meet your intellectual, health and social post-ownership desires and develop a plan for achieving them.

Chapter 4

How Much Money Do You Need?

ONCE YOU'VE IDENTIFIED the exit strategy that will fulfill your business objectives and created post-ownership personal goals, the next big question is, "Can I afford the lifestyle I enjoy today and fulfill my future aspirations after I sell my business?"

The rule of thumb in financial planning is that an owner's post-ownership life will cost 80 percent of what it did when running the business. This is a very broad stroke rule, and every business owner's post-ownership plan is different.

If your goal is to retire, recognize that we are living longer and more actively than our predecessors, which, of course, drives costs up. You may end up needing more money to live your retirement life than as a business owner since you will have the time to travel and do whatever it is you desire.

The 80-percent rule also assumes that you'll be in a lower tax bracket. Taxes are always subject to change, however, and the unprecedented low capital gains tax has nowhere to go but up, which will take a big bite out of the investment income intended to pay for your retirement.

You've spent years juggling the financial demands of running a business. You don't want to exit it, only to discover that you're now going to struggle financially. It's not uncommon for a business owner to underestimate their post-ownership financial needs. Yet the last thing we want to tell a client is that instead of flying to see the grandkids four times a year, they're only going to be able to see the kids twice a year and... they have to take a bus! A post-ownership plan integrated with a financial plan will ensure this doesn't happen to you.

One of the major contributors to post-sale regret is that the owner had insufficient financial planning performed prior to the sale. Then they subsequently discover they don't have enough money to replace the income they had previously received from their business.

To understand our client's post-ownership financial needs, we perform a thorough financial analysis and create a goal-based personal financial plan. This process begins with collecting and organizing the financial resources available to fund your life post-ownership.

What Do You Have? (Income)

Identify all sources of income:

- Savings and investments, such as traditional IRAs, Roth IRAs, brokerage accounts, tax-deferred accounts, 529 college savings plans, or employer-sponsored accounts, like a 401(k), 403(b) or 457 account.
- Retirement income, such as a pension, income annuity, alimony, royalties, rental property, HSA or Social Security benefits.
- Insurance policies, such as life insurance with cash value.
- Other assets, including real estate investments, collectibles, an inheritance or personal property.
- Business value.

You need to understand the value of all available assets that may fund your financial goals, including the potential sale of your business.

In most financial plans, the business will be the largest asset.

According to the Exit Planning Institute,
85–90 percent of the wealth of a privately held
business owner is tied up in their business.[7]

Business owners often think they know the value of their operation. They may know someone who sold their business and then based their projected value on their friend's experience, even though their friend's company may be in a completely different industry. At times, they overvalue their business because it's emotional and their "baby" that they've nurtured for many years. An owner may also undervalue their business because they don't understand the process for valuing it.

In the next few chapters, I'll discuss business valuation in detail. Note that your financial plan will require a market valuation of your business (for mergers and acquisitions, or M&A, purposes). This is different from a valuation used for legal purposes (for example, estate planning).

Successful exits involve owners who view their business as an asset and meticulously create transferable value as it matures. They understand the importance of engaging a team that provides an objective valuation early on and continue to keep an eye on value as they make critical decisions.

Valuing your business is not a onetime exercise only undertaken when you decide you're ready to go to market. Think about it, you check your investment account at least once a month when the statement is issued. Wouldn't you also want to understand the change in value of your business as it grows, an asset that is likely larger than your stock portfolio, perhaps even considerably larger?

With a clear understanding of the business's market value, you're then able to reconcile the degree to which a liquidity event will contribute to your financial assets.

A valuation will also inform you and your team of the best exit strategy to meet your business and financial goals. In most cases, a sale to a third party will result in the highest price.

Many business owners dream of a family succession. That is, until they pencil out the deal and realize that they can ill afford the family discount that was factored into the price.

> **In Sam's case** in the previous chapter, he paid market value for the business when he purchased it from his father. Yet he knew when it was his turn to exit, a strategic buyer would pay a higher price than a transfer to the next generation would have commanded.
>
> Although he had a daughter who worked in finance and expressed interest in the business, he understood that fourth-generation businesses statistically have a 95 percent failure rate. "If the business fails under the next generation, there goes my retirement and my kids' inheritance. If they want a business, I'll buy them one," he said, reflecting on his decision to sell to a third party.

The ultimate value of your business will always be what the liquidity event produces upon exit, and this is the big unknown for many business owners. But an M&A market valuation will provide the necessary information to integrate the business's value into your financial plan.

Once you've determined your income sources and calculated the expected future income available, you'll then need to understand the cost of your life goals.

What Do You Need? (Expenses)

In the previous chapter, you identified your post-ownership goals, and perhaps you identified some of the following ambitions:

- **Travel:** Trips that you want to take annually or a trip of a lifetime.
- **Major purchases:** A boat, plane, motor home, or hot-air balloon.
- **College:** A plan for you to go back to school or fund the grandchildren's education.
- **Home:** A vacation house or your dream home in a special location.
- **Family care:** Fulfilling the need to care for parents or other family members.
- **Special events:** Weddings, vow renewals, bar mitzvah, or bat mitzvah.
- **Donations:** Gifts or bequests upon death.
- **Entrepreneurship:** Starting another business.

With your goals identified and the associated expense quantified, a complete budget for all personal liabilities and living expenses can be created.

Living expenses include:

- **Basic living expenses:** Mortgage, equity line, real estate tax, insurance, HOA fees, utilities, trash, water, lawn and maintenance, cell phones, internet fees, clothing, groceries and dry cleaning.
- **Insurance:** Disability, health, life and long-term care.
- **Cars:** Insurance, maintenance, fuel, personal property tax, parking and tolls.
- **Entertainment:** Dinner out, an evening with friends, and don't forget club fees.
- **Miscellaneous:** Gifts, childcare or support, hobbies and pet care.

Health care may be one of your largest expenses post-ownership. If you believe, based on your health and family history, your estimate will be beyond what a Medicare supplement will provide, be very conservative in your projection since health care costs will continue to rise. According to the Fidelity Retiree Health Care Cost Estimate, an average retired couple may need approximately $300,000 after tax to cover health care expenses in retirement.[8]

Another key consideration when carefully budgeting the cost of your post-ownership life is that often a privately held business owner will run personal expenses through the business. So it is important to give careful consideration to the true financial benefit received from the enterprise. It's advisable to look back a minimum of three years and identify all personal benefits afforded to the owner. We've seen it all in our practice—cars, cell phone bills, health care, meals and entertainment, personal travel, HOA fees, private planes, equestrian dues, personal home construction, and more.

Most business owners grossly underestimate their post-ownership life, so be very astute in forecasting your needs. The business may provide a significant contribution to an owner's lifestyle that will need to be replaced, and it's critical to uncover any income replacement gap.

Once you've calculated your income and expense requirements, you'll understand any gap in your financial resources that will prohibit you from meeting your goals. This insight will drive your decision as to when to exit your business. If there is a deficiency, you have two choices:

1. Go to market, get the best price you can, and alter your post-ownership goals to reflect what is possible with the financial resources available.
2. Optimize the business and continue to monitor the value and market conditions to determine the appropriate time to exit in order to meet your goals.

We at Legacy Partners use a goal-based financial planning system that takes into consideration actuarial tables, inflation rates, and tax rates, as well as stress testing investments for bear market conditions. We provide extensive financial planning so every client understands their financial position *before* and *after* they sell their business. We also have best-in-class wealth management partners who guide our clients' investments to produce the highest return while mitigating the tax impact in order to protect their financial future.

We will explore the question of whether to go to market now or to hold and optimize in "Chapter 9: Do You Sell or Do Your Grow." But first, you'll need to understand how a business is valued, which we'll cover in "Chapter 8: How Risky Is Your Business?" Next up, though, it's time to meet the team of professionals who will create and execute your Master Exit Plan.

TAKE ACTION

- Hire an exit planning advisor (such as Legacy Partners) to create your MEP and calculate the market value of your business.

- Use your financial statements to identify all your financial resources, then create a conservative budget for future expenses.

- Work with the advisor creating your MEP to ensure they have the necessary data for your financial plan. That way, you can get a clear picture of your financial position before and after your business potentially sells.

Chapter 5

Who Can You Count On?

T O SELL A BUSINESS, you need a multi-disciplined approach to ensure that you're well represented by an M&A team and that, upon the liquidity event, your wealth is protected. The success of your sale will hinge on the ability of your team to negotiate the highest price and best terms, protect you from liability exposure post-close, mitigate taxes, invest your proceeds, and safeguard your wealth through proper estate and family planning. It's not just about the onetime sale event.

The holistic approach we take at Legacy Partners toward developing a Master Exit Plan for our clients is comprehensive. We act as the team leader, or quarterback, and work with best-in-class professionals representing the disciplines necessary to execute your exit strategy: M&A advisors, transactional CPAs, M&A attorneys, wealth managers, estate planners, specialized insurance professionals, and family governance specialists. A lack of expertise in any of these disciplines will result in diminishing your wealth whether now or in the future.

When a business owner begins the process of selling their business, there are always three fundamental questions to address.

1. Who can help me?
2. When is the right time?
3. What is the process?

This chapter answers the first question. Subsequent chapters will address the remaining ones.

The thought of selling a business, which may be the owner's largest asset, is often met with fear. Business owners hesitate to sell while they wrestle with the questions:

- What if I do the wrong thing?
- What happens to my employees if I sell to the wrong buyer?
- What will I lose if I'm taken advantage of?
- Who do I trust?

It always comes down to trust, and your first task will be to identify the right team members to help you through the sale process. For a privately held business in the middle market, the traditional options come down to a business broker, an investment banker, or a mergers and acquisitions advisor.

I've had hundreds of conversations with business owners confused by the different types of professionals who can help them sell their business.

Here's the breakdown for what most business owners see as their only choices to help them get a deal done.

- **Business brokers** traditionally serve smaller companies with less than $1 million in EBITDA. These companies tend to be owner-operated lifestyle businesses, such as a single-location or virtual service business, a franchise, or a convenience store. They're often sold to individual investors as opposed to a financial or strategic buyer. A broker may not require a retainer but will take a percentage of the sale at closing called a success fee. This is similar to selling a home, with a similarly passive approach. They typically lack the reach that an investment banker or an M&A advisor will have in sourcing buyers and rely mostly on funding a deal with a Small Business Association (SBA) loan or seller note.

- **Investment bankers** are financial advisors who provide an array of financial services, including raising capital for companies (both debt and equity) and assistance with M&A transactions. For instance, if you need to expand your manufacturing facility, they can facilitate a bond issuance, or they may raise equity financing by taking a company public. They also advise in valuing businesses and assist in the process of a sale. There are different levels of investment banks: bulge bracket, middle market, and boutique. Classification depends on the size of the bank and the size of the deals they handle. The smallest of investment banks are regional boutique banks. They work on smaller M&A deals in the $50 million to $100 million range, whereas the bulge bracket banks will serve the larger $100 million (and more) deals. Investment banks handle complex transactions that are highly regulated, which is reflected in the retainer fee required to engage them. Investment bank professionals are also required to hold licenses to meet SEC requirements.

- **M&A advisors** are the middle ground between a business broker and an investment banker. Whereas the business broker deals with smaller companies and investment bankers fulfill the needs of large complex transactions, M&A advisors engage with companies that most often fall between $1 million and $50 million in EBITDA transaction value. They may provide sell-side and buy-side representation, corporate finance, and growth advisory services. The degree to which an advisor is licensed depends on the services provided and the structure of the transactions they support. Typically, an advisor will require a retainer fee, which will be less than that of an investment banker. An M&A advisor and an investment banker are both proactive and competitive in their approach to selling a company. Their goal is to drive value and engage with multiple strategic and financial buyers.

If your strategy is to sell your business to a third party, ask yourself these three basic questions to guide you in determining which advisor will serve you best.

1. **What size transaction value are you anticipating?** If your business is less than $1 million in EBITDA, then a business broker would be right for you, or you could potentially list your business for sale on your own. If your business is between $1 million and $50 million in EBITDA, an M&A advisor is the right choice. Larger, complex transactions above the $50 million EBITDA mark may benefit from working with an investment banker.

2. **Who would the potential buyer be?** If the most likely candidate is a local competitor, then a local broker would be a fit. However, if you feel your business could attract a PEG, family office, or national strategic buyer, then your exit planning advisor will align you with the right M&A advisor or investment banker. If you think an internal transaction, such as a management buyout, family succession or ESOP,

could fulfill your exit goals, then an exit planning advisor will align you with the appropriate specialists to guide you in the execution.

3. **How much help do I need?** If you don't feel that you need help to normalize your financial statements, understand value, market your business, evaluate buyers, or negotiate the deal, then selling your business yourself and working with a transaction-oriented attorney to finalize your transaction could be the right choice. If your business truly is a lifestyle business and your EBITDA is less than $1 million, using a local broker who will help you identify buyers and negotiate the deal would be the right strategy. However, if the business is above the business broker EBITDA threshold, an M&A advisor is the preferred choice because they will drive the selling price by attracting and engaging multiple buyers.

Deciding to sell your business can be daunting, and many times, a business owner is tempted to go it alone. The primary reason they state is to save money. Successful entrepreneurs are by nature risk-takers and feel they are good negotiators. They've also been successful in building a business, so they think, "Why can't I figure out how to sell my business? I've been smart about it. I've sold a house before, so surely I can do this too." But can you?

I've yet to meet a business owner with EBITDA greater than $1 million who has the time and expertise necessary to execute a successful exit on their own. Your business will be better off with you concentrating your time and attention on pushing the business to a higher level while working with a seasoned professional who will focus on the sale. A consultant is worth the dollars invested in executing the sale of your business.

Identify Your Best-in-Class Team

So, what's the right choice that will best serve you, the business owner, and only you?

Exit Planning Advisor

The first advisor you'll need, regardless of the size of your business, is an exit planning advisor who will be your quarterback. An exit planning advisor is completely independent and will provide you with unbiased advice on creating a comprehensive exit plan that addresses not only the business exit strategy and execution, but also the financial and personal implications.

All the potential team members mentioned earlier—business broker, investment banker, and M&A advisor—have a stake in the game. They each will make money from the sale of your business, and you must be astute in assessing whether they're working toward what's best for you rather than them. Your exit planning advisor will help you choose the best option to represent you in the sale of your company and will shepherd you through the entire process.

To exit your business and transition to the next phase in your life successfully, there are other considerations beyond the liquidity event that need to be addressed, such as tax mitigation, your future financial plan, estate planning, and your post-ownership strategy.

Legacy Partners, as exit planning advisors, values a business and creates an optimization plan to address any weaknesses that diminish the marketability of a company. Then, with a better understanding of the value of the company and the financial expectations of the business owner, we design an exit strategy and establish our clients with the appropriate M&A advisor to execute the sale.

In some instances, depending on our client's industry, we may also execute the sale as their M&A advisor. We oversee every step of the transaction to ensure our client's best interests are served at the highest level. By providing independent advice within a holistic framework that considers an owner's business, personal and financial objectives, we ensure an owner exits with ease.

One of the most frequent comments we get from our clients is that we relieve them of the burden of managing the process themselves, allowing them to do what they know best—run the company. It's enough that you know the ins and outs of your industry. You don't need to be an expert in selling a company as well. Hire someone to take control—an advisor who will bring best-in-class specialists to guide you through every aspect, ensuring you'll get the best terms when selling your business.

At Legacy Partners, we efficiently manage the entire process, taking our clients from equity to liquidity so they can "stick to their knitting," as the British would say, without unnecessary distractions.

Most business owners work with a multitude of advisors.

- A CPA to ensure tax compliance and provide accounting support.
- A lawyer for any real estate transactions, collection issues, contract negotiations, and so on.
- An insurance agent to protect the business in myriad ways, from physical to employee retention programs.
- An investment advisor to protect and grow their wealth.

These professionals and their specific disciplines are critical to the success of a business. Always keep in mind that your advisors are specialists in their respective fields, and you hire them for their expertise. You wouldn't have heart surgery performed by a dentist. Nor would you have your taxes prepared by your wealth manager. So, when preparing to exit your business, you'll need an exit planning advisor who specializes in M&A and can coordinate these advisors.

As you go through the process, your exit planning advisor will collaborate directly with your other advisors, taking you out of the middle and allowing you to focus on running your business.

We had a client who was given a valuation by their CPA, who advised them not to go to market because the value was a lowly $8 million based on the book value from the company's financials—liquidation value. Book value doesn't take into consideration any of the qualitative characteristics or intangible assets that drive future revenue. It's a snapshot in time. Our client ignored the advice and ended up with a $26 million offer for 80 percent of their company from a PEG.

A CPA without M&A business valuation experience could be dead wrong and cost a business owner the deal of their lifetime. We've also had CPAs almost derail deals over the tax impact. You will never get around paying taxes, but if you have a transactional tax specialist on your team, they will mitigate the taxes as much as possible.

Your exit planning advisor will complete a valuation, advise you on optimization strategies to close any value gap, create an exit strategy, and advise you on the impact of the sale on your personal financial plan. Then, you'll also need the following additional team members to guide you through the sale of your business.

M&A Advisor

Depending on your sector, the purpose of your exit strategy, and the size of the potential transaction, your exit planning advisor will recommend a business broker, investment banker, or an M&A advisor who's experienced in your industry and has existing relationships with buyers.

In the M&A arena, it is also critical to understand that there are buy-side and sell-side advisors—those representing actual or potential buyers and those representing you. Could an M&A advisor be in the pocket of a buyer? Yes, and an independent exit planning advisor will ensure this doesn't happen to you.

How Two Owners Saw the Light

In the two stories that follow, you'll meet different business owners who attempted to sell their companies on their own. They came to realize, though, that their peace of mind and net proceeds were well worth the advisory fees.

> **Paul** owned his business for decades and was considering retirement when he received a call out of the blue from an intermediary who represented a buyer interested in purchasing his company.
>
> "Why not check it out?" he thought. "A conversation can't hurt."
>
> He had several meetings with the prospective buyer set up by this representative. The buyer and buy-side representative wined and dined Paul. Conversations dragged on for months with no progress except a lot of information being shared with the potential purchaser—a strategic buyer pursuing a synergistic fit.
>
> Eventually, realizing that the deal was going nowhere and worried about the information he'd divulged about his business, Paul engaged Legacy Partners to represent him. A formal auction process with the engagement of multiple buyers began, and the original buyer bowed out as soon as they understood there were other interested parties.
>
> A buy-side representative will contact you directly and may try to fool you into thinking they have your best interest at heart. Often they're industry experts and will have their finger on the pulse of the market in your sector.

So don't be afraid to put them on the spot. Ask them, "Who's paying you?"

If the answer is that they're working on buyer mandates, it means they're representing a specific buyer or a buyer they expect to emerge from their network. Please understand that they are representing the buyer and will never go to bat for you. The buyer they're working for is looking for a proprietary deal and expects to be the only suitor. No competition always equals a lower price.

In Paul's situation, the buyer was strategically slowing the deal in the hope that the price would also come down.

There's also a significant risk in giving away too much information too soon. Being chatty with the buyer is never a good thing when selling your business. I like the old 80/20 rule for meetings—listen 80 percent of the time, speak 20 percent. The timing and context in which information is disclosed for our clients is very carefully planned and monitored.

Another common mistake when a seller engages directly with a buyer is to answer the question, "What's your price?" When a seller names their price, they've set the ceiling. If a buyer names the price, they've just set the floor.

Paul ultimately realized he had no control—certainly no leverage—and needed representation from a team that was solely on his side if he were to secure the best deal. Having engaged our team, his deal eventually closed, several million dollars higher and with much better terms than the original buyer had offered.

Many business owners believe that since they've been successful in running a business for years, they're capable of selling their business on their own. They consider themselves great negotiators, having sharpened their skills with vendors, customers and employees. However, negotiating an M&A deal is a completely different ballgame and better left to the pros.

A buyer also approached Sam, the wine cork owner, directly. Sam had purchased thirteen companies to grow his first business through an acquisition strategy, relying on his CPA and attorney to help close the deals. He thought to himself, "I can sell my company on my own."

At the same time, sitting on a letter of intent (LOI) and unable to sleep at night, he nervously thought, "This business is my largest asset and I'll probably sell only one in my life. This actually is a big deal!"

He tried to save money by not hiring a professional. But at the eleventh hour, as the deal was close to finalizing, his worry about the price won out.

With proper representation, Sam discovered that the LOI that was keeping him up at night wasn't even remotely in the right ballpark. The advisory fee he paid to execute his deal, by contrast, was "worth every penny for a substantial increase in price and the accompanying peace of mind."

Certified Public Accountant

According to the 2019 Small Business Finance and HR Report, 86 percent of small business owners who engage with an accountant agree their CPA is their most trusted advisor.[9]

The relationship between a business owner and accountant is very personal. Knowing someone's finances is equivalent to seeing them naked. Your accountant keeps you out of hot water with the IRS and other taxing authorities. They also know if you're paying alimony, and if so, to how many exes. It's a deeply intimate relationship. Therefore, it's natural to turn to your CPA for advice as your business grows, matures and eventually your focus turns to exiting.

As mentioned previously, most accountants do not have the expertise to guide you through the exit process. However, they will be deeply involved in various stages of your transaction.

From the initial stages of developing your exit strategy, your advisors will rely on your CPA for guidance in understanding financial statements and tax returns as they value the business. Your accountant will help in identifying all discretionary or extraordinary expenses that are unnecessary to running the day-to-day operations during the valuation process.

At the close of your deal, the biggest bite will be taken from the IRS. There are multiple ways to structure your deal, and this decision has an enormous impact on your tax liability. I've spoken to CPAs who've told me about clients who sold their businesses without speaking to them during the process. They learned about the sale when the client came in to do their year-end taxes, and the lack of the CPA's involvement cost the client millions.

Nothing will exasperate a CPA more than being left out of your impending deal. As a bonus, going it alone will most likely cost you in unnecessary taxes being paid to that silent partner of yours—The United States Treasury!

Once you have an LOI in hand, it's time to run the numbers. We have strategic partners who are M&A transaction tax experts. They create a tax impact analysis to help us guide our clients in analyzing offers and negotiating with buyers.

Wealth Manager

Upon the close of your deal, the settlement funds will be wired to a wealth manager who is prepared to execute an investment strategy reflective of your risk tolerance and needs.

I spoke with a wealth manager at a conference once who shared a story about a client of hers who sold his business. The funds were wired to her to be placed in a cash account. Millions of dollars were invested in cash with a minuscule return. She told me she was having trouble getting him over the shock of his sudden wealth, which made it difficult to move him to invest the funds at a rate of return that would grow his portfolio.

Being an entrepreneur is high risk, so I'm always a bit amazed by how skittish an owner can be when it comes to investing their sale proceeds.

We've all heard the stories of people who win the lottery, have no investment advisor, and pivot back into poverty within a very short period. It also happens to business owners who've sold their businesses for millions of dollars and don't have a wealth management strategy in place at close.

Often a business owner thinks that creating a business plan, growing the business, and then selling is the entire cycle. The investment world is complex, and a relationship with a trusted wealth manager is critical to the success of your financial future.

We work with our clients' wealth managers, or recommend one if they don't have one already, to ensure the liquidity from the sale grows and is properly protected.

Estate Planning Attorney

Advisors joke that people spend more time planning a vacation than they do their estate plan, but it's no laughing matter. I guess it seems bothersome to tend to something that pertains to us after we're dead.

For a business owner, however, it's a bit more complex. Proper estate planning will protect your business while you're alive, as well as ensure the distribution of your assets after your death per your wishes and in a tax-efficient manner.

There are five key components to a business owner's estate plan.

1. **Living trusts:** A living trust is a legal entity that ensures that your assets, including the business, are kept out of probate and allow a confidential transfer

of ownership. If properly done, a trust will enable your business to continue without you and will minimize the tax impact upon transfer. You may also consider a testamentary trust or charitable trust in your estate planning.

2. **Durable or limited financial power of attorney:** A durable power of attorney allows you to appoint one or more persons to act wholly on your behalf if you become incapacitated. A limited power of attorney agreement empowers an agent to act only on specified activities, such as for financial reasons.

3. **Medical power of attorney or advanced directives:** Often referred to as a "health care proxy," this allows you to designate one or more people to make health care decisions on your behalf if you should become incapacitated.

4. **Will or pour-over will:** A will provides instructions for the disposition of your personal property and appointment of a personal representative to settle your estate. A pour-over will ensures that assets not previously funded into a trust are, at the time of death, automatically transferred or poured into your previously established trust.

5. **Life insurance:** There are a multitude of reasons to have life insurance as a key component of an estate plan, including the assurance that your family will be financially secure upon your death. It's also used to fund buy-sell agreements and to retain key employees. Insurance can be used to balance out estate dispositions when trying to divide equally between children who may or may not work in the business. A policy can also be borrowed against making it a funding source for the business. Customized policies, such as private placement life

insurance, offer substantial tax efficiencies and wealth protection benefits to business owners.

At the end of your life, your estate plan will protect your business and your heirs. We find that this is the part of an exit plan that's most ignored and often in need of updating.

Without a sound estate plan, your assets may be disposed of in a means contrary to your wishes. There also may be huge tax burdens that could have been easily avoided. And I hate to even spell this out for you, but proper and specific estate planning can ensure that your family doesn't go to war over your business when you're gone.

M&A Attorney

In conjunction with receiving an LOI, a transaction-oriented attorney's assistance will be key to closing your deal. The M&A world can be contentious, and a good M&A attorney will protect you from any future liabilities while helping to review and execute both the LOI and the definitive purchase agreement (DPA). Selling a business requires expertise in contract and tax law, estate planning and, depending on the structure of the deal, securities, as well as regulatory issues. Don't make the mistake of hiring the lawyer responsible for your collections as your primary legal advisor for your exit process.

We had a client who insisted that his friend be retained as his deal counsel. The friend happened to be a bare-knuckle litigator not used to navigating difficult contractual matters. If your attorney's mindset is predisposed to wanting to win a case versus negotiating a business deal that's mutually beneficial to both sides, in all likelihood, there will be no deal. We protected our client by insisting they engage an experienced M&A attorney, who strived for a win-win scenario while protecting him and moving both sides to a successful close.

Jonathan Kim, JD, MBA, is a leading mergers and acquisitions attorney who oversees all client transactions for Legacy Partners.

I interviewed Jonathan about working with an M&A attorney, and he shared the following insights.

Chris. At what point in the process should an M&A attorney be introduced?

Jonathan. Ideally, an experienced M&A attorney should be brought onto the field in the first inning and not as a closer. M&A attorneys who've handled numerous deals are adept issue-spotters. They can help to reduce deal friction and transaction costs by identifying and addressing potential liabilities early on and anticipating roadblocks that might delay or scuttle a deal. In addition, fundamental decisions are often made at the beginning of the M&A process, such as the overall structure for the transaction—decisions that may have a significant impact on the economics and risks associated with the deal.

The earlier your M&A attorney becomes involved in the planning and negotiation of any threshold issues—even if final agreement over the economic terms of the deal is left to others—the greater the probability that your deal will close successfully, on time, and with more money in your bank account.

Chris. A buyer's attorney will draft the offer, which is presented in the form of an LOI. The seller then needs an attorney to review the LOI. What are the key components of that document?

Jonathan. Fair-minded M&A attorneys can differ on the most important components of an LOI. It is more than a bullet-point term sheet outlining an offer to purchase a business and a stepping-stone to a definitive purchase agreement that will embody the final terms of the transaction.

The parties should clearly identify which provisions of an LOI are intended to be legally binding. At the same time, LOIs are generally intended to be nonbinding agreements—meaning they spell out the intentions of a buyer and seller to enter into a final agreement for the sale and purchase of a business—and the parties should expressly state this nonbinding intention. Failure to state in unambiguous terms which portions of an LOI are binding and which are not could inadvertently commit the parties to certain deal terms before a DPA is fully negotiated, agreed and signed. In my opinion, a comprehensive LOI should address both binding and nonbinding provisions.

Nonbinding provisions typically spell out the overall nature and structure of the acquisition. This encompasses deadlines for key milestones, like the completion of due diligence, and contingencies, if any, such as the buyer securing financing, before the parties will proceed to a DPA.

There are critical items that will need to be addressed, including the price and terms, the business to be acquired, liabilities to be assumed, the allocation of assets, due diligence, indemnification obligations, key contracts, post-sale employment agreements, consulting contracts, non-compete and nonsolicitation agreements, and the escrow of funds.

The price, or aggregate consideration, a buyer is willing to pay will likely be the most important issue for the client. But the terms and conditions governing how the buyer will pay for a client's assets and business will be equally important. For example, will the buyer require financing, and if so, how much? Will the seller receive all cash at closing or will a portion of the consideration be held back via a seller's note or an earn-out?

When identifying the business to be acquired and liabilities to be assumed, it needs to be more than a statement that the deal will be an all-asset or a stock sale. In addition to outlining which portions of the seller's balance sheet the buyer will acquire, other questions should be addressed, such as whether the price will include net working capital. Also, how will inventories be handled, including any work-in-progress? And what about cash and accounts receivable? Will the seller keep them to pay off any existing liabilities?

The asset allocation for the transaction will need to be reported to the IRS by the seller's accountant. The way in which the purchase price of the business is allocated across asset classes can affect the tax rate imposed on the sale, perhaps significantly, since different classes are taxed at different rates.

It's important that the buyer describe the process and actions that will be undertaken during the deal's due diligence phase. Requests may be made for financial documents, copies of key contracts, and other information required to assess the value of business assets and the cost of existing or potential liabilities.

Expectations regarding nonfinancial terms that will be included in the DPA, such as indemnification provisions, may also be covered in an LOI. While the details may be left to the final deal documents, the general scope of the seller's indemnification obligations to the buyer may be spelled out here.

The nonbinding provisions should also identify any third-party consents needed for key contracts necessary to run the business following a sale. In addition, many buyers will want sellers to stay on for some period post-sale to assist with transition issues. The general terms of any required employment or consulting arrangements should therefore be defined.

A seller may want to work in their industry again in the future, and if so, a buyer will want to control how soon they may face the seller as a competitor. So, it's important to establish a noncompete agreement. The same applies to nonsolicitation considerations if a buyer is concerned that current employees might be enticed by the seller to leave in conjunction with a sale.

Lastly, a buyer may want a percentage of the overall sale purchase price held in escrow for a reasonable period to cover any costs guaranteed under the indemnification obligations undertaken and the representations and warranties made by the seller in the DPA.

As for the binding provisions of the LOI, it's common to find information related to expectations of confidentiality, exclusivity and termination clauses, transaction expenses, and the governing law for dispute resolutions.

It's critical to specify that the LOI and its contents will be subject to any existing nondisclosure agreements (NDAs) or, if no NDA is in place, that the terms of the LOI and any information shared between the parties will be kept confidential. Nothing will torpedo a deal faster than a failure by either party to keep a lid on their intentions.

A buyer will want a period of exclusivity where the seller will not attempt to negotiate with another party. At the same time, a seller will want to ensure that the LOI and its exclusivity provision have a definitive expiration date. That way, they can either agree to extend the date or move on if no deal is to be had.

The LOI should also address how transaction expenses will be allocated between the parties. For example, each party may agree to bear all expenses incurred for its own benefit, such as legal and accounting fees, while agreeing to share mutually beneficial expenses, such as filing fees.

Lastly, the LOI will specify the governing law for dispute resolution. Typically, this is a standard boilerplate provision that spells out the procedure for resolving any disputes that may arise under the LOI and the governing law for such disputes.

Chris. How does an M&A attorney assist in negotiations?

Jonathan. Many M&A attorneys will not be active participants in the negotiation of the deal's business terms (unless the client believes their involvement is vital to the process). However, they will take a leading role in the negotiation and drafting of the DPA and any related agreements. While standing in the background, they may also advise clients on negotiating tactics prior to the DPA stage, such as during the LOI or due diligence processes.

In any case, many of the key components of the DPA must be negotiated and agreed upon before they're committed to writing. These include the who, what, when, where and how of the deal: as in *who* will be the actual parties to the agreement, *what* assets and liabilities of the business will be acquired or retained, *when* will the conditions to closing be met and the price paid, *where* will the closing occur, and *how* will the consideration for the deal be paid (for example, in cash or newly issued shares).

It's at this stage that an experienced M&A attorney with plenty of "been there, done that" under their belt proves his or her worth. A client simply cannot afford to have someone learning on the job during the sale of their most valuable asset, and quite possibly the deal of their lifetime.

Chris. What is the attorney's role in due diligence?

Jonathan. From the seller's perspective, their M&A attorney can assist in the due diligence process by helping to make it as smooth and transparent as possible for the buyer's counsel. After all, the buyer is typically interested in purchasing the bulk of the seller's assets and business, if not the entirety. The last thing they—or the seller, for that matter—want is any surprises that will affect the price a buyer is willing to pay for the company.

Before the parties get to the LOI phase, buyers will have performed some financial diligence. Potential buyers, naturally, will want as much information as they can get as early as they can get it for valuation purposes. However, access to the data room typically does not occur until the LOI is signed.

When it comes to a diligence data room, a good M&A attorney, in conjunction with your M&A advisor, will get things organized well in advance of granting full access to a buyer and their advisors.

Chris. In addition to the DPA, what other documents will your M&A attorney review?

Jonathan. If you have an experienced M&A attorney who you turn to regularly on other matters, ideally, he or she will have helped you to prepare your standard NDA in advance of any exit transaction discussions, as that will help set the stage for such discussions.

In addition to the DPA, your attorney may be asked to review a broad range of other documents, some prepared previously by the seller's in-house counsel or other outside counsel (for example, employment agreements) and some drafted by the counsel for the buyer (for example, noncompete or nonsolicitation agreements).

Unless they're experienced in the area, M&A attorneys may need to look to specialists when it comes to reviewing particular documents. Patents, trademarks and various intellectual property (IP) documents, for example, may require analysis by attorneys well versed in the field as part of a valuation exercise or to help avoid any challenges to IP rights by third parties.

CHRIS. How does an M&A attorney help facilitate the closing process?

JONATHAN. Your deal counsel can help facilitate the closing process primarily by making sure all the moving pieces mesh together smoothly and that the many tasks appearing on the deal closing list are accomplished as set out in the DPA. A veteran M&A attorney will know how to reset expectations if deadlines are in danger or are missed.

Moreover, provided they have a good working relationship with any in-house counsel and the buyer's counsel, they'll be able to come up with creative solutions when obstacles arise. These would be solutions that are mutually acceptable to the parties involved and which successfully address the business objectives of both sides while limiting, to the extent possible, the seller's legal liability.

Again, this is where troubleshooting experience on the part of an M&A attorney can be worth its weight in gold when the closing of a deal is hanging in the balance.

CHRIS. What are some issues that can delay closing or potentially prohibit a deal from closing?

JONATHAN. Failure to adhere to the original timeline for the deal is the most common delay. Of course, there may be good reasons for extending the closing date, such as items outside the control of the buyer and seller (for example, regulatory approvals).

Contingencies that arise during due diligence can also push back the timeline, including matters like environmental or hazardous waste remediation problems not previously known to the buyer (or seller).

Failure to understand potential tax consequences of a deal can also delay or prohibit it from closing. That's why it's best to involve both M&A attorneys and accountants familiar with such issues early on, so any bombs can be defused and minefields successfully navigated.

CHRIS. What are some ways that an M&A attorney can help in containing closing costs?

JONATHAN. One way is for the seller to begin by utilizing an exit planning and M&A advisory firm, such as Legacy Partners, that collaborates with someone like me who oversees a nationwide network of M&A attorneys. To help minimize outside legal costs on M&A transactions, I identify suitable co-counsel to handle all legal and dealmaking services and then oversee their work during their representations.

I source the co-counsel from my extensive network of lawyers and law firms that I have built over the past thirty years. They are typically partners who trained at some of the best law firms in the country's top legal markets like New York City, Chicago and San Francisco. Since then, they've founded their own boutique firms, often in cities with smaller legal markets where the bulk of the deals they handle involve small to medium-sized companies.

These boutique firms have lower overhead—and by extension lower billing rates. By staffing with small teams, they're further able to minimize costs.

Alternatively, I look to branch offices of national law firms. These are usually located outside the country's major legal markets and therefore have lower rates, but they also have access to experts throughout the firm's locations.

In either case, the client benefits from having experienced co-counsel (the firm I retain on behalf of the client) handle the nuts-and-bolts of legal work associated with the deal. They also have an even more experienced lead counsel (me) who understands all aspects of M&A deals and can ensure that the client is getting top advice and legal services at a lower cost than with most large law firms, even factoring in my fee.

Creating your Master Exit Plan will require a best-in-class team of experts who specialize in each part of the process.

An exit planning advisor should be your first hire and will provide you with unbiased advice throughout the entire transition. They will serve as your quarterback and manage every step in the development and execution of your plan. They will also recommend experts, help you select your team, and will continuously collaborate with the team you put in place.

Again, your success will hinge on the quality of the experts you hire, so be wise in your choices.

TAKE ACTION

- Identify those advisors whom you already work with who are qualified to fill the necessary roles and be part of your exit team. Keep in mind, a successful exit requires expertise in mergers and acquisitions, taxes, M&A law, estate planning and wealth management.

- Consult your exit planning advisor to recommend experts needed to fill any gaps in creating your Master Exit Plan.

- Discuss with your exit planning advisor as to what type of M&A specialist you require to execute the sale of your business (business broker, M&A advisor, or investment banker). Your exit planning advisor will then recommend the appropriate transaction team for you.

MASTER EXIT PLAN
STEP II

Understand Your Business Value
and Optimization Opportunities

Chapter 6

Will Your Business Attract a Buyer?

According to the International Business Brokers Association (IBBA) *2019 Market Pulse*, advisors decline about 70 percent of the business opportunities that come their way because the business is considered "non-saleable."[10]

THE VALUATION PROCESS will include a qualitative analysis that will uncover opportunities to optimize the business and close any value gaps. Qualitative analyses are often referred to as strengths, weaknesses, opportunities and threats (SWOT) analyses. When assessing each of these areas, note that strengths and weaknesses are internal to a business, while opportunities and threats are external.

These qualitative characteristics fuel a buyer's risk assessment when determining their required ROI to invest in a business. The risk factor reflects the discount rate used when computing the business value during the quantitative analysis. We will go into discount rates in more detail in "Discount Future Free Cash Flow" on page 96.

The lower the perceived risk, the higher the perceived transferable value and the amount of premium that is paid for a business. Successful entrepreneurs grow a business cognizant of increasing transferable value by decreasing risk (and thus the discount rate used in the valuation). This drives the value and ultimately the price when the business goes to market.

As a business owner considers making the decision to sell, the question is, "Has the owner created a business with transferable value that a buyer can capitalize on to meet their ROI expectations?" (Meaning, they'd be willing to pay a lofty price for it.)

Most privately held business owners tend to believe that value is driven solely by profit. They focus on increasing sales and margins, and cutting expenses. I often hear the 5x5x5 rule from owners. They believe that if they increase sales by 5 percent, increase margins by 5 percent, and lower sales, general and administrative (SGA) expenses by 5 percent, they've increased value. But it's not that easy.

The solution isn't simply growing sales and margins and decreasing expenses. There are many other factors to consider.

We had a client with $63 million in revenue, $14 million EBITDA, and no debt on the books. They were analyzing the impact of taking on a new customer that would add $10 million in revenue. Would the additional sales volume increase the business marketability in the eyes of a buyer?

Projections showed the increased sales would strain the operational capacity, requiring a capital infusion to expand operations and resulting in adding debt to the balance sheet. Also, there was no evidence of economies of scale. Costs were not going to decrease with more units sold, so margins would not increase.

As a result, the valuation financial model showed a decrease in transferable value.

The above case study is a great example of how an increase in sales would only result in an increase in demands on the business's infrastructure and employees. It would simply create more headaches for the business owner with no increase in profitability or transferable value.

To increase the transferable value of a business, it's critical to focus on the many qualitative factors that drive profitability, growth and the strength of an organization. This will result in a higher selling price for the owner.

For your qualitative analysis, you'll want to assess the quality of your business's eight primary transferable value drivers:

1. Strategic plan
2. Management team and human capital
3. Sales process
4. Marketing plan
5. Operations
6. Finance
7. Legal
8. Contingency plan

Strategic Plan

When a buyer is considering investing in a business, a key consideration is if a strategic plan is in place to scale or expand easily without a major capital outlay. Buyers want assurance that the business can grow and increase revenue, resulting in a corresponding increase in profit to meet their ROI target.

A buyer will evaluate the current business growth plan, including how well-defined the target market is, the potential for growth, and whether the business can easily accommodate the projections.

Years ago, when Oprah featured products on her show, the good fortune bestowed on these highlighted businesses was referred to as the "Oprah Effect." However, many of the businesses experienced a high failure rate because the operations weren't capable of fulfilling the increased demand sparked by appearing on the show. In dealmaking, this is referred to as the "winner's curse."

Investors also need to understand your value proposition against competitors, how your competitive advantage is leveraged, and if there are any barriers to entry. They'll want to determine whether your business is resistant to commoditization or disruption. For example, technology, capital requirements, regulatory—anything that will give them protection against increased competition. Also note, since an optimal buyer is always looking for "best-in-class," they'll research your business reputation, so be sure your company delivers impeccable results.

Your strategic plan should include a projection for growth and be supported by specific tactics to achieve the goals that are tied to clear key performance indicators (KPIs).

Management Team and Human Capital

A well-developed management team assures an investor that the business is not owner-dependent and that if you, as the business owner, are no longer part of the equation, the business will continue to expand.

When an entrepreneur launches a business, they wear all the hats necessary to run the enterprise. Successful entrepreneurs tend to have that "control freak" characteristic, which is great at the beginning as they establish their foundation. However, this characteristic is not a benefit if the business is still dependent on the owner when it's time to exit.

As the business matures, the CEO must have a bird's-eye view and not be concerned with micromanaging operations, but instead remain focused solely on growth strategies, innovation, brand extension, and delegating. The only way for that to happen is to give responsibility to people who have the right skills.

Human capital is one of the most valuable intangible assets of a business. So much so that investors will buy companies purely for their people. These transactions are called "acqui-hiring," which means hiring the best people through an acquisition.

If your exit strategy is to sell your business to a third party, the quality and depth of your team will determine the success in meeting that goal. A team has depth when there are multiple people within the organization who can fill each role. So, if you lose a key person, business operations can still continue because you have other individuals with suitable experience, skills and certifications to step in. Leaders who understand the vision for growth and have the skills to execute the plan are critical to the value of the business and a successful transition.

An investor also needs assurance that when they scale the business, they'll have a team in place to support its growth that is appropriately incentivized to stay.

Sometimes, as a business transitions from start-up to maturity, people are kept in roles that they're not necessarily suited for, and this misalignment devalues a business.

A valuable organization has the right *people*
in the right *place* at the right *time*
with the right *skills* at the right *price*!

We had a client who left the business for six months to take care of an ill family member, and the business kept ticking along with no negative impact on operations or results. If an owner can take a month off and the business continues to run, we know that company is not owner-dependent.

Many business owners have learned from unexpected events, like the COVID-19 pandemic, that having a succession plan for key roles is an important component of their management team contingency plan. The ability to be agile in the face of disruption always centers on the skill of the management team to recover from shocks.

Here are a few of the questions you need to ask when assessing the depth and quality of your team.

- What would happen if you lost a key employee?
- Do you have a plan in place to develop new talent continuously?
- Is your corporate culture supportive in developing new leaders?
- Do you have a reward and retention plan for key employees?

Sales Process

Future predictable revenue from which a buyer can receive a return on their investment is the gold standard in dealmaking.

Revenue sustainability proves to an investor that the business will be able to fund future growth through current cash flow. Be mindful of your growth rate and use your working capital efficiently.

Working capital measures the company's operational efficiency and short-term health. It's important to strike a balance. A buyer doesn't want to see liquidity issues where they feel they'll need to invest heavily to realize growth potential. Conversely, an investor will see excess reserves as underutilizing capital that could be used to support growth.

Assessing the sales process as a driver of business value involves looking at the:

- **Sales strategy:** An effective sales strategy is aligned with the overall growth plan and is supported by a sales team with clear goals, objectives and a tactical plan that will drive revenue.
- **Sales team:** The depth of the sales team and their capacity to generate growth either in customer acquisition, new product lines, or expanding markets is key to revenue growth, as is an appropriate compensation

plan. Not every incentive plan is a good one, and we've seen businesses that continue to move the goal post on their sales team, which is very demoralizing and non-productive.

- **Sales projections:** Exploring sales projections, conversion rates, margins and pricing for each customer and product line can be an eye-opener for a business owner. A sales analysis may uncover low-margin customers who should be fired and replaced with higher quality customers. I know that's hard to do. We've had many owners say to me, "Any paying customer is a good customer." But we've often found that the lowest margin customers are the ones that monopolize your sales team's time, prohibiting them from being successful in servicing higher margin, higher revenue customers.

- **Revenue character:** Not all revenue is weighted equally in the eyes of a buyer. For example, being paid post-project isn't as attractive a model as the customer who pays upfront or incrementally for your service or product.

The real gold standard will always be recurring revenue.

Predictable revenue = lower perceived risk by the buyer = a higher premium paid upon exit

---

Demonstrated recurring revenue streams drive the price for a business upward. Here are a few examples.

- Service contracts
- Automatic renewal product, service or content subscriptions
- Strong customer retention rates
- Recurring royalties

In addition to analyzing each customer's contribution to your gross margin, an investigation into your competitors can also reveal any opportunities for price elasticity.

There are only two ways to increase sales revenue: increase price or increase volume. Increasing volume to maximum operational capacity is always a goal, but understanding pricing for your product is somewhat vague and not something you want to make a mistake on. Overprice your product, and a business can terminally suffer. Underprice it, and you're leaving money on the table and devaluing the business.

Understanding your customer, your costs, and your competitor's pricing will provide guidance as to the price the market will bear for your product or service.

Buyers also are sensitive to customer diversification. Most investors don't like to see more than 15 percent of revenue coming from a single customer and are mindful of the percentage of sales driven by the top three customers. This presents a conundrum for an entrepreneur who wants the big whale of a client in their industry. The fastest way to grow is to get the big client, right? It's risky in regard to the value of your business because if the big whale jumps ship and a chunk of revenue is lost, the business is back to square one in terms of customer development. Better to attract minnows that will grow, allowing your organization to stay well diversified.

Marketing Plan

A robust marketing plan that presents the strategy to grow sales gives an investor confidence in future growth and potential return on investment. In the small- to middle-market, 50 percent of companies have no written marketing plan.

Too often, a business owner's marketing is ad hoc and opportunistic. We had a client who responded to our inquiry about his marketing plan by saying, "I think we have a Facebook page!" Not quite what an investor's looking for.

A marketing plan is the blueprint to deliver sales results and includes:

- A clear marketing strategy that's aligned with the overarching business strategy and goals.
- A marketing team with a defined budget.
- A marketing position statement and defined target audience.
- Branding that relays the organization's value proposition in relation to the competition.
- A tactical plan to execute the marketing strategy and KPIs to assess the plan's success.

A well-defined marketing plan will enable the owner to make meaningful decisions and grow the business without wasting resources.

Operations

An investor's process of analyzing operations will depend on the industry the business is operating within. Manufacturing, retail and service are all assessed with varying parameters.

The manufacturing analysis will focus on production efficiencies and whether a business is operating under lean principles. In retail, an investor will focus on the movement of inventory. The service industry operations focus on a front end that delivers the service to the customers and the back end that produces the product.

Regardless of industry, every business needs a written operational strategy. Additionally, well-documented systems and procedures will lower the perceived risk by assuring an investor that the business can operate without the owner in it.

Finance

Your finance team adds tremendous value if properly staffed and leveraged. The accounting department has a reputation for being immersed only in historical data, ensuring proper reporting and compliance, cutting costs, and so on. However, they're not just transaction-oriented.

A well-developed finance team understands the entire financial picture of an organization and is a key player in developing a strategy to grow a business. They proactively manage the need to secure capital for growth, oversee risk management, advocate for new technology to streamline operations, and ensure efficiencies across departments through process improvements. They're perceived to be only in the background, but in reality, as the keepers of the data, they are a focal point of driving business success.

I've seen my share of accounting departments that are staffed with bookkeepers whose title changed to Chief Financial Officer as the company grew without the corresponding increase in knowledge. Having a qualified finance team with the appropriate experience for your business stage will give an investor confidence that your financial strategy will support future growth and that your financial planning, analysis and reporting are complete and prepared in accordance with Generally Accepted Accounting Principles (GAAP). Clean financials will increase a buyer's confidence in investing in your business.

If your company has more than $2 million in EBITDA, audited financials will be worth the cost of supporting the validity of your financials. If your financials are not audited, reviewed is the next best option, as opposed to internally generated.

Legal

People often laugh when we ask them if they've ever been convicted of a felony, but legal is no laughing matter when selling your company. The investor will want to know if you or your business have any negative history with the law. They'll also want to be aware of any threatened or pending litigation and the potential outcome.

Beyond keeping your business current with all filings and licenses, a good legal team will have your contracts and agreements buttoned up and all intellectual property protected.

We had a client who was in due diligence when a vendor threatened a patent infringement lawsuit after our client began to manufacture a product that was previously purchased through the vendor. Their patent attorney was pivotal in assuring the buyer that the lawsuit had no legal merit.

Good legal advice is worth its weight in gold and can save your deal.

Contingency Plan

A business can face many crises both internally and externally. A key employee leaves suddenly or becomes ill, a supply chain disruption, key customer departure, or a data breach are a few internal headwinds. Externally, we've all faced a pandemic and the resulting fallout. There are also hurricanes, floods, fires, disruptive technology, industry pressures, economic forces, changes in government policy or regulation, and other unanticipated disturbances.

Contingency planning allows for immediate activation when a business faces an unforeseen circumstance, which will minimize disruption to operations. Preparing for unpredictable events will protect the business from threats to its viability.

The key is to minimize risk and potential chaos with appropriate planning. Not only will a buyer feel more secure in the value of your business if he has assurance that the business and employees are properly protected, but you'll also have greater peace of mind knowing that you have a plan.

The above drivers are all intangible assets that add value. It is important to document your intangibles, including any intellectual property, your operational procedures, how technology is utilized within your business, the marketing strategy that drives sales, customer service protocols, financial controls and procedures, preferred customers, vendor lists, and the approach used to identify, attract, train and retain new talent.

Identify, document, protect and defend your intangibles.

The qualitative characteristics of your business drive the risk factor, and therefore the multiple of EBITDA, an investor is willing to pay for a business. Note that the multiple of EBITDA paid by a buyer is the inverse of the discount rate, so if you decrease the risk in each of the above eight drivers of transferable value, the multiple paid for your business when sold will increase.

TAKE ACTION

- Your exit planning advisors will engage in a qualitative analysis when they value your business. However, as your business matures keep a pulse on the characteristics of your company that add value. Perform a SWOT analysis to help identify areas of improvement.
- Don't buy into the thought that more revenue is all that matters. Analyze each of the eight value drivers in your business (strategic planning, human capital, sales process, marketing, operations, finance, legal and contingency planning) and augment them as needed.

Chapter 7

What's Your Business Worth?

MOST BUSINESSES BEGIN with one simple goal: to make money. Yet, most fail. There are a variety of reasons. The market for the product or service isn't as big as initially perceived, or the capital required to launch and scale fully is underestimated. There might be a lack of skilled team members or ineffective marketing. Often, there is no strategic plan in place to ensure the business is agile in the face of a constantly changing global environment. And there are many other reasons as well.

Successful businesses, like Matt's in our first chapter, cycle through various stages from launch to growth, then maturation of transferable value, and eventually an exit that harvests the wealth. Transferable value is the cornerstone of a business owner's MEP, and the selling price received upon exit will depend on all the decisions made by the owner that either increased or decreased the business's value.

I mentioned earlier that the ultimate value of your business will always be what a buyer is willing to pay. Consequently, every MEP begins with a valuation exercise so, when you do sell, you'll have a realistic expectation of what the market will bear. You wouldn't sell your house without reviewing comparable sales in your area from a Realtor. So why would you sell your business, which is potentially your largest asset, without first understanding what the value is?

In using that analogy, I don't mean to compare selling a house to selling a business, as it's a bit of an apples-to-oranges scenario. A house is a tangible asset that we use for a particular purpose. We live in it. A business, however, at the root level, is a collection of intangible assets that are used to create future cash flow. Since selling a tangible asset requires a completely different process from selling one with both intangible and tangible assets, don't assume you understand one simply because you've done the other.

Quantify Your Business Value

A business valuation is based on past performance, potential future revenue, and the quality of intangible assets. The sooner you understand the value of your business, the better prepared you'll be to exit successfully. If you wait until the day you decide to retire or receive an offer, you'll be way behind the proverbial eight ball, and most often, it is too late to execute a successful sale.

Let's first recognize that there are many reasons to value a business.

- **Raising capital:** An entrepreneur who's looking to raise capital to support growth will need to present the value to potential investors.
- **Acquisition strategy:** A business owner looking to grow through an acquisition strategy will need to assess not only the value of their business but also the value of the target business and the value of both combined.
- **Increase transferable value:** As a business matures, every owner needs to be sure that the focus of their

efforts, capital and expertise is centered correctly to ensure the business is growing in a meaningful way. This will prevent misplaced resources and the potential of having the ladder leaning against the wrong wall at the end of the day, prohibiting your business from being sold.

- **Legal purposes:** Throughout the life cycle of a business as well as for personal reasons, an owner will need a valuation specifically used for legal purposes, such as a buy-sell agreement, partner dissolution or buy-in, divorce resolution, estate tax planning, or an employee incentive program.

- **Transactional:** The most common reason today, due to aging demographics, is that the owner is preparing to sell their business and retire. As mentioned in "Chapter 4: How Much Money Do You Need?" on page 41, understanding the amount available to be invested post-sale is an important factor in creating your financial plan.

There's a great deal of confusion about business valuation, and unfortunately, that alone stops business owners from properly preparing for their eventual exit. It's critical that you understand the process that should be used to assess the value of your business. If you have no idea what the value is when you receive an offer, how will you know if it's a good offer or if a buyer is trying to steal your business out from under you? You won't.

A professional valuation must be performed when you're preparing to sell your business so you understand whether going to market will meet your financial objectives. It's not as simple as valuing a public company, which is done by multiplying the number of shares outstanding by the share price to compute the market capitalization.

Valuing a private company is far more complicated, and unfortunately there's no simple formula. I've had business owners lament that they'd spent thousands of dollars for a valuation and were presented with three different results that were so diverse the numbers were completely useless.

Business valuation is also confusing because not only are there many reasons to value a company, but also many types of value.

- **Enterprise value or fair market value (FMV):** Arm's-length value garnered in the open market based on the assumption that the buyer and seller are both fully informed and neither is under duress.
- **Investment value:** The value to a particular investor.
- **Strategic value:** The value placed by a synergistic investor.
- **Fair value:** Independent value used for financial reporting or legal purposes.
- **Book value:** Calculated as assets – liabilities. This is used for liquidation purposes.

As M&A advisors, our focus when preparing our clients to go to market is on enterprise value. Understanding the enterprise value of your business will:

- highlight gaps in value and serve as a guide as you make critical decisions about growing your business.
- serve as a guide as you assess the optimal exit strategy to meet your financial goals.
- help you assess the best time in the maturity of your business to go to market.
- disclose any due diligence issues that will prevent the successful sale of your company.

If your valuation uncovers that you cannot afford to sell the business because you have a significant value gap compared to what you need financially for your post-ownership life, you'll either need to hold and optimize your business for a future sale or adjust your future financial needs.

The valuation process is a complicated topic and begins with a quantitative analysis, or in layman's terms, "crunching the numbers."

There are four basic approaches to calculate the value of a privately held business.

1. The income approach
2. The market approach or comparable company analysis (CCA)
3. The asset approach
4. The rule-of-thumb approach

The Income Approach

The income approach includes discounted cash flow (DCF) or capitalized historical cash flow analysis. Since DCF transforms measures of cash flow into estimates of value using discounted projected cash flow, it is considered the most in-depth approach.

I'm going to focus on discounted cash flow, as that's most often used when forward projections are available and we're preparing to take a client to market.

The computation includes the following steps:

1. Normalize the financial statements.
2. Discount future free cash flow.
3. Compute residual value.

Let's take a closer look at each of these.

Step 1. Normalize the Financial Statements

This process includes assessing trends, understanding variances in financial statements, and normalizing the prior three years plus the current year financials. This is done through recasting, which focuses on adjusting EBITDA for non-cash, extraordinary and discretionary expenses.

EBITDA gives an investor a clearer picture of the operational profitability of a company and enables them to make a more accurate assessment when comparing investment opportunities. It allows a buyer to layer on their own tax burden per their business structure and any interest, based on their chosen capitalization of the company.

$$\text{EBITDA} = \text{Earnings} + \text{Interest} + \text{Taxes} + \text{Depreciation} + \text{Amortization}$$

Earnings are your net income from operations. *Interest* is added back to net income because how a company is financed differs from business to business. The same goes for *taxes,* as there are different tax structures, so we want to add taxes back to your earnings. *Depreciation* and *amortization* are then added because they're non-cash expenses.

"Adjusted EBITDA" refers to expenses that are added to or subtracted from your EBITDA through the recasting process for all extraordinary and discretionary expenses.

Extraordinary expenses include nonrecurring expenses, such as a severance package, a lawsuit settlement, a bad debt, or a loss on the sale of assets beyond what is normal and customary.

Discretionary expenses are personal expenses, such as meals and entertainment, travel and nonworking family payroll, included in the financials for the sole purpose of minimizing a business owner's tax burden. While discretionary expenses are within the boundaries of deductibility per the Internal Revenue Code (IRC), they're not necessary to operate the core business.

Note that discretionary expenses put through your financials over the years of ownership to reduce your tax burden are, in reality, slowly selling off your company. How, you ask? Because you're taking profit along the way, and a buyer will never accept all our addbacks, no matter how aggressively every penny is defended. In essence, you're receiving payment for your business through tax reductions over the years.

We've seen it all in our practice, from private planes to equine expenses—and no, the owner in question was not a veterinarian. It's up to you to decide whether you want to receive full value upon exit or take a discount by slowly selling off your company over time. It's best to present your business running efficiently with the most profit by reducing discretionary expenses when you prepare to go to market.

Adjustments can also decrease EBITDA. (For example, under-market rent paid to a related entity must be adjusted to reflect market rent properly.) Owner's compensation may also be above or below market and need adjustment.

When recasting the financial statements, the balance sheet, in addition to the income statement, is also reviewed for adjustments. Working capital is just as important as EBITDA in an M&A deal. A buyer will require normalized working capital to operate the business.

Working Capital = Current assets − Current liabilities

This is most often done on a debt-free, cash-free basis, meaning that debt and available cash are not included in the calculation. The valuation process will verify that the assets and liabilities are fairly stated. (For example, the value of inventory and collectability of accounts receivable are accurate, and all liabilities, including contingent liabilities, are correctly included and quantified.)

A business owner is often surprised how the normalization process positively affects the value of their business. If this step in the valuation process is overlooked, the business value will most likely be suppressed, which will result in a less than optimal purchase price from a buyer.

At Legacy Partners, we guide our clients to look deeply into their discretionary line items. If your business sells for a 5x multiple, every dollar is worth $5 in your pocket. That means that $100,000 of positive adjustments equates to a $500,000 increase in purchase price. Note that all adjustments must be defendable and the more addbacks, the less credible the financials will be viewed by buyers, which may result in a prolonged due diligence period and a price or terms adjustment.

Step 2. Discount Future Free Cash Flow

Now that we have adjusted the EBITDA and understand the true profitability of the business for the current year and prior three years, our focus shifts to the future. Noting that an investor is buying a business to receive an ROI, the next step in the calculation of value will include a five-year forecast of the future cash flow the business will generate. This is illustrated in a pro forma financial statement. The projection is then discounted back to the present value to account for the time value of money.

IRS revenue ruling 59-60, 1959-1 CB 237 — IRC section 2031 is one of the most commonly cited rulings regarding the valuation of a privately held business. The following key element of the ruling sums up the importance of future projected revenue in assessing value.

> Valuation of securities is, in essence, a prophesy
> [*sic*] as to the future and must be based on facts
> available at the required date of the appraisal.

Free cash flow is simply the cash a company generates that's free to pay creditors or fuel growth after taking into consideration cash outflows, such as capital expenditures, taxes and changes in working capital. Depending on how the company is capitalized, we may use free cash flow to the firm, or we may compute free cash flow to equity, which takes interest payments and borrowings into consideration.

When computing the discount rate to be applied—also called a hurdle rate—a company's weighted average cost of capital (WACC) may be used or the "Build-up Method," which is more common and takes into consideration the risk-free rate of return, equity risk premium, size of the company, and the company's specific risk in determining the discount rate. The qualitative assessment of the eight primary value drivers presented in "Chapter 6: Will Your Business Attract a Buyer?" on page 77 will influence the company's specific risk.

The discount rate is a reflection of the buyer's perception of how risky the deal is and ultimately represents their expected ROI. To equate value to multiples, a discount rate is the inverse of the multiple a company could potentially receive going to market. For example, a 20 percent discount rate = a 5x multiple.

Step 3. Compute Residual Value

The last step requires the computation of terminal or residual value because, beyond the five-year projection, the company still has value for the investor.

To compute this value:

1. Estimate the annual percentage rate at which you expect your cash flows to grow beyond the last year of your discounted cash flow analysis and add this to 1. (For example, a 2 percent growth rate would be 1.02.)

2. Multiply this number by the forecasted annual cash flow from the final year of your discounted cash flow analysis to determine the cash flow in the next year.

3. Subtract the annual growth rate from the discount rate you are using in your discounted cash flow analysis.

4. Divide the cash flow from step 2 by the number computed in step 3.

The result is the residual value.

The income method to value a company is very complex and requires significant financial modeling experience. If your company has recurring revenue, which makes cash flow predictable, this approach is an appropriate method to assess value.

The Market Approach or Comparable Company Analysis

The market approach method compares your business to the prices that investors have paid for other similar companies.[11] For example, a financial buyer, such as a private equity group, may use a business's average trailing twelve months (TTM) adjusted EBITDA to establish the price they are willing to pay based on a multiple the market is bearing.

Another market approach is to compare public company values in a sector and discount the value to reflect the difference in liquidity for a private company. This approach, however, may be difficult to apply to smaller businesses in the lower middle market. Due to the smaller size, there may be relatively few transactions to draw a comparison from to arrive at an accurate conclusion of value.

The Asset Approach

The asset approach assesses the value of each individual asset on a business's balance sheet as if they are being liquidated or replaced.

There are two primary methods to determine a business's value using the asset approach, but since both are very subjective, neither are recommended as the sole method for a rigorous quantitative analysis. Instead, the asset approach should be used in combination with the other methods.

A common asset approach used to value a business for liquidation purposes is book value, or assets minus liabilities. However, this is not an appropriate method to determine the value of a company that is marketable.

Another asset approach to determine intangible value is the excess earnings method, in which excess earnings are capitalized and then added to the tangible asset value to compute the total firm value. This method was developed by the US Treasury Department to determine the intangible value of distilleries to compensate brewers and vintners for their losses during prohibition. Note that there's quite a bit of estimation and subjectivity in this formula, so you may want to take it with a grain of barley!

The Rule-of-Thumb Approach

Establishing a business's value using the rule of thumb is simplistic in comparison to the above methods and is based on market rules (formulas) within specific industries. Some sectors are sold exclusively using the value established by this valuation method. For example, a physician's practice typically, by rule of thumb, is valued at 1.0–1.25 times earnings.

> A professional valuation will encompass a mix of the above approaches and will be dependent on the industry in which the business operates. It's complicated and is based on assumptions and estimations that can change by a hair. I wish it were as easy as valuing the market capitalization of a public corporation, but unfortunately, a simple formula doesn't work in the private sector.

Beyond the method, the quantitative analysis of financial statements also involves the assessment of KPIs. The four main categories include:

- **Liquidity ratios,** such as the current ratio, quick ratio, and operating cash flow ratio, are used to determine a business's ability to pay off short-term obligations.

- **Solvency ratios** measure the percent of a business's after-tax income (net profit plus depreciation) available to cover short- and long-term liabilities.

- **Efficiency ratios,** such as total assets and inventory turnover ratios, measure a company's ability to convert assets or leverage them into revenue.

- **Profitability ratios,** such as return on assets or equity and profit margins, compare the business's earnings to expenses.

These metrics are compared to the company's previous periods, other companies, and against industry standards in assessing the value of a business. Industry-specific benchmarks may also be used, for example, sales per square foot for a retail establishment.

There's always a push-pull dynamic between what a seller feels the value is and the reality of the market. When we at Legacy Partners value a business for M&A purposes, we use several valuation methods and analyze market data to establish the range in price that a business could potentially receive.

When you sell and reap the reward for all the years of dedication and hard work in building your company, the value of the business will ultimately be what the open market will deliver. This will be driven by the caliber of your team guiding you through the process, the buyers they bring to the table, and the price investors are willing to pay.

TAKE ACTION

- Work with your exit planning advisor to calculate your business's value from a mergers and acquisitions perspective.

- Include the business value (minus estimated taxes and selling expenses) in your personal financial plan. Then assess the viability of meeting your business, personal and financial objectives by selling your company.

MASTER EXIT PLAN
STEP III

Assess Your Business Risk

Chapter 8

How Risky Is Your Business?

WHEN CREATING a client's MEP, we frequently find weaknesses in a business's asset protection plan. For example, they have inadequate insurance, or their buy-sell agreements are not in place, haven't been funded, or haven't been updated in years. In my experience, most businesses are the largest asset in a client's personal financial plan, and it is vitally important that proper measures are taken to protect the goose that lays the golden egg.

COVID-19 struck a nerve by demonstrating how important business continuity planning and risk management are. A well-strategized contingency plan ensures the business will continue in the face of disruption and reduces risk for the organization. In turn, this increases the enterprise value of the company and the potential for a successful sale. Mitigating risk significantly improves enterprise value in the eyes of all buyers.

Always expect the unexpected because from time-to-time something will go wrong, and COVID-19 will not be the last unforeseen challenge for businesses.

Statistically, privately held companies are the most unprepared when havoc strikes. Their contingency plans and risk management are most often nonexistent or, at best, inadequate. They're too busy running day-to-day operations and putting out fires. With their head in the sand, they often think nothing will ever happen to threaten the viability of the business. Ask any business insurance professional and they can tell you all kinds of "I can't believe this happened to me!" stories.

Business owners were caught off guard with the COVID-19 pandemic and nobody could have predicted the ensuing fallout. Of course, those with a continuity plan and proper insurance in place, such as business interruption insurance, fared far better than those without.

A comprehensive plan requires that stakeholders stress test the business and explore all potential risks, both internal and external. I encourage you to dream up some worst-case scenarios that could derail your business. Identifying potential issues is the first step. While you're at it, ask your employees from all departments what they see as potential risks that could cause a major trip-up for the operation. We often find that employees think of situations related to their contribution to the business that an owner might never imagine.

Once each potential negative impact has been identified, brainstorm how to mitigate or protect against the risks and create a written contingency plan to ensure the business will recover quickly.

Many weaknesses may be identified, including capital deficiencies, supply chain or customer concentration, cybersecurity, and other limitations. In the previous chapter, we discussed how these factors devalue a business. This chapter explores disruptions that can destroy a business and how a proper insurance strategy can protect and increase its value.

According to the Exit Planning Institute,
40 percent of all privately held businesses do
not have a plan that covers a "forced" exit.[12]

There are five "Big D's" that can kill a business: death, disability, departure, disaster and divorce. These situations can dramatically alter the ownership and value of a company and require solutions.

- If you, a partner or key employee were to die or become disabled unexpectedly, is the business properly protected?
- Does your business continuity plan have a provision for disability?
- If there is a disagreement among partners, are you prepared for dissolution?
- If there is a disaster, is your property and business interruption insurance adequate?
- Would your company survive a divorce that includes an asset buyout to a spouse?

To guide you in understanding the strategies you can deploy in developing a plan that will protect your business from the five D's, Jeff Carey offers his insights. Jeff is an expert in business continuity planning and a strategic partner of Legacy Partners, providing guidance for our clients on how to protect the value of their businesses. He's also a partner with Vertex Planning Group, part of the Commonwealth Financial Group, a Boston business and personal financial services company specializing in risk protection and wealth management.

Buy-Sell Agreements

A buy-sell agreement is a legally binding document that requires one party to sell their ownership interest to another party following a triggering event—one of the five D's.

Mary co-owned a business for decades, and just when she and her partner were on the cusp of selling it to retire, her partner suffered a fatal heart attack. There was no buy-sell agreement in place, so she became partners with her deceased partner's three sons. Her new partners didn't want to sell the business, which left her in a precarious financial position that dashed her retirement dreams.

A properly executed buy-sell agreement would have protected Mary and will protect your business from succumbing to many of the five D's.

Here's my interview with Jeff Carey regarding the value of buy-sell agreements.

Chris. What's the benefit of having a buy-sell agreement?

Jeff. Formal buy-sell agreements are common for businesses with multiple owners, as they are designed to eliminate ambiguities as to exactly how things would be handled among the various owners in the event of some sort of catastrophic scenario relating to one of the five D's.

Chris. Does a business owner who doesn't have a partner or family member in the business still need a buy-sell agreement, and if so, why?

Jeff. Buy-sells are quite common with both single-owner and family-owned entities and can be hugely beneficial in terms of protecting all parties involved.

Essentially, these arrangements are like traditional buy-sells, only there isn't a mutual obligation to purchase among all parties, meaning there's only a one-way obligation to transfer the business should a particular triggering event occur.

As an example, let's say you have a single-owner entity with two key employees. In this instance, the owner may elect to create a one-way buy-sell that would allow for the transfer of the business over to both key employees in the event of his or her premature death or disability. This would allow for the ongoing continuation of the business and would typically entail economic considerations for the decedent, and potentially heirs, depending on the specific triggering event.

Ultimately, the benefit of this type of arrangement is twofold, since you're economically protecting both employees and loved ones.

The same method is often applied in family business scenarios, especially if the goal for the family is primarily to ensure that wealth is handed down to the next generation. For example, you may have a scenario where a husband and wife each maintain a 40 percent share of a family business and they have two children who each possess 10 percent stakes in the company.

When designing a buy-sell for this type of situation, one may opt to have one-way buy-sell agreements between each parent and the kids. This would allow for the shares to move to the next generation, but not create an obligation for the senior generation to buy out their children if something were to happen to them. Typically, you would round out this strategy with a special arrangement between the siblings to address their respective ownership stakes, using a different type of arrangement, such as a cross purchase buy-sell agreement, which I'll discuss more later. (See page 111.)

In some instances, depending on a variety of dynamics, it may be simpler to use traditional estate planning techniques to address intergenerational transfer issues.

The bottom line is, it's very important to coordinate this type of planning with both your tax and legal counsel to ensure optimal outcomes.

Chris. What are the mechanics of a buy-sell agreement?

Jeff. There are a few moving parts to consider. At a high level, a formal buy-sell agreement is a legal document.

It should outline all the details in terms of what would happen to the organization, owners and their respective family members if a triggering event were to occur.

A well-constructed buy-sell agreement should clearly lay out and define all potential triggering events, as these events often create a legal obligation to transfer shares. It's paramount that these events be defined to ensure that there's congruency between one's buy-sell agreement and personal estate plan.

There are several additional elements to consider. The first one is valuation. What is the mutually agreed upon value of the organization today, and equally important, what will be the mutually agreed upon valuation formula moving forward?

If there's a funding component to the overall agreement, which customarily would consist of a combination of insurances, a clear explanation is needed of how insurance proceeds would be used if a triggering event were to occur. Furthermore, the document should address how things would be handled if no funding was available and a triggering event occurred.

Most of what I've discussed thus far could be defined as the foundational, mechanical elements of a buy-sell agreement. There are many other considerations regarding which sort of clauses may make sense to include in an agreement. Things like clawback provisions, tag-along options, bad boy/girl considerations, noncompetes and discounting triggers. Without getting too far into the weeds here, I'd say this...

A lot of times, I see scenarios where buy-sell planning gets addressed in a minimalist way. There may not be a detailed stand-alone document, but rather a brief paragraph or two of buy-sell language embedded into the operating agreement. My stance is this: something is better than nothing.

However, such a minimalist approach is generally better suited for an upstart with limited value—for example, an idea that started in a garage with a handshake, so to speak. Once a company begins to mature and generates significant cash flows, it's incredibly important for owners to coordinate with their tax, legal and business advisors to come up with a thoughtful and detailed agreement that properly protects all interested parties in a comprehensive way.

Chris. What are the options for structuring a buy-sell agreement?

Jeff. There are two main options, as well as a hybrid. The first would be a cross-purchase style agreement. This simply means that if there are two owners of a business, they each agree that if one were to pass away, the other would buy out the decedent's shares.

A variation of this style of agreement would be a trusteed cross-purchase, which would include trust language as well as a third-party disinterested trustee, who has a fiduciary responsibility for ensuring that the specifics of the agreement are carried out as intended should a triggering event occur. This variation is common when there are multiple owners. It can help ease administration, particularly with agreements that are funded with insurance.

The second structure to consider would be an entity purchase plan, sometimes referred to as a "stock redemption agreement." The key difference here is that if a triggering event were to occur, the company itself would be buying the shares rather than the other owners.

The last option is the hybrid, or as it is often referred to, the "wait-and-see buy-sell." This type of arrangement does not declare the exact structure upfront and allows for the decision to be made after a triggering event.

When attempting to determine the optimal buy-sell structure, there is a host of considerations. Most revolve around taxes, which vary based on the type of business entity. I know it's a recurring theme, but again, the optimal selection process should involve a detailed discussion with an organization's tax, legal and business advisors to ensure that agreements are constructed in the most appropriate fashion.

CHRIS. How is a buy-sell agreement funded?

JEFF. Buy-sells are often backed or funded by a risk management portfolio consisting of various types of insurance. This could include things like buy-sell life insurance, disability buyout protection, and key-person coverage. In addition to specific product selection and coverage amounts, it's critically important to ensure proper ownership and beneficiaries are selected. Failure to do so could result in significant and unnecessary tax obligations should a triggering event occur.

CHRIS. What if one partner is uninsurable?

JEFF. There are a few options, depending on the specific type of coverage that one is seeking to procure. In some instances, a principal may have underlying conditions that would eliminate them from consideration as it relates to disability coverage, but it's entirely possible those issues would have no bearing on the procurement of life insurance.

Practically, if someone is not what an insurer would consider an ideal risk candidate, or worse, completely uninsurable, there are alternative strategies that should be considered.

One possibility might be guaranteed issue coverage. This can sometimes be procured through a group insurance offering, where all employees are given some form of insurance coverage—let's say, life or disability, with either simplified or guaranteed underwriting. Oftentimes, there may also be some options for carving out owners and giving them higher coverage amounts. While this can be advantageous, coverage amounts are limited, and it's rare that someone could procure the fully desired coverage using this strategy. Nevertheless, it can certainly be a good start.

There are also industry-specific plans that are available for certain types of professionals, where they can procure limited amounts of coverage, again with simplified or guaranteed underwriting.

Once simplified or guaranteed underwriting options are exhausted, there are other strategies to consider, such as procuring increased coverage for healthier owners. For instance, let's assume you have three partners seeking buy-sell life insurance coverage. If one of the partners is uninsurable and the other two are perfectly healthy, one consideration may be to increase the amount of permanent, cash-value-accumulating life insurance coverage. Over time, this would create a sinking fund within the organization. If down the road, the uninsurable partner were to pass away, the surviving partners could access the cash values inside of their respective policies to assist with a down payment for the pending buyout.

Another thing to keep in mind is that if all options have been exhausted, and one partner is still significantly underinsured relative to the others, it would likely make sense to review the buy-sell document carefully and consider potentially extending the duration of payment terms for the un- or underinsured's estate.

For instance, in the event of death, there may be language that states any obligated buyout value that exceeds insurance proceeds would be paid to the decedent's estate over five years, with some stated interest rate formula. For any partners with limited or nonexistent insurance coverage, those terms could be extended to, let's say hypothetically, ten years to avoid negative cash flow implications that could impede the safe, ongoing operation of the entity.

CHRIS. How often should a buy-sell agreement be reviewed?

JEFF. Approximately every one to three years as a general best practice. A lot will depend on structure.

In some cases, the agreement may require that all owners convene annually to restate the mutually agreed upon valuation for the business. In such instances, an annual high-level review would be warranted.

These agreements should also be reviewed if there are potential pending changes, such as the retirement of a current owner or perhaps the inclusion of a new owner.

CHRIS. What are the tax considerations?

JEFF. As discussed, buy-sell planning should be a team effort, and tax advisors need a prominent seat at the table. Candidly, some of the biggest mistakes I've seen are when legal counsel drafts the document in a silo and fails to communicate with tax counsel.

One of the most important elements from a tax perspective is properly understanding the nuanced differences between a cross-purchase agreement and an entity purchase agreement, and how each option works based on one's corporate structure.

Failure to understand the options could lead to a missed opportunity in terms of a step-up in basis upon an owner's death, and thus, lead to unnecessary taxes being paid down the road once the business is sold by the surviving partners.

CHRIS. What is the risk of not having a funded buy-sell agreement?

JEFF. Put simply, the risk is potential economic duress for all parties involved. It's important to note that buy-sell planning protects the business, the owners, and their respective families. Closely held businesses are wonderful things. Most fulfill some sort of societal need, while providing economic livelihoods for the owners and employees.

A funded buy-sell agreement provides much more certainty of outcome should a triggering event occur and better protects all parties involved. For example, let's look at two simple scenarios, one with funding and one without.

Let's say there's a $10 million company fully owned by two equal partners and one of the partners suddenly passes away. There's an unfunded buy-sell that states the surviving partner must buy out the decedent's estate over ten years in equal installments. In this scenario, the decedent has a spouse who would receive ten annual payments of $500,000, not including any interest obligations.

Let's examine a few other considerations that might also come into play. Under this scenario, the spouse is now left to hope that her deceased husband's business partner can successfully run and maintain business operations for a period of ten years without the help of his longtime friend and visionary partner.

In addition, a healthy chunk of the installment payments is likely being spent by the spouse as they come in as a substitute for the deceased partner's lost salary.

Alternatively, had this agreement been funded with $5 million of life insurance on each partner, then the surviving spouse would be receiving a lump sum. Ultimately, this would alleviate long-term operational risks and create a more beneficial financial scenario that would potentially allow for the spouse living off the interest of the lump sum instead of spending it as it comes.

Meanwhile, the surviving partner would be left in much better financial shape going forward as there's no longer a $5 million debt obligation on the balance sheet.

General Insurance Considerations

The number of insurance claims in the United States due to natural disasters is increasing. Every part of the country experiences severe weather events—wildfires, tornadoes, hurricanes, avalanches, earthquakes, snow and hail. Protecting your operation against a catastrophe with proper insurance will ensure your business is able to recover quickly, which will safeguard its value.

Again, Jeff Carey provides the following insights:

CHRIS. From an overall protection standpoint, what are additional insurance coverages that a business owner should consider?

JEFF. From a continuity planning perspective, business overhead insurance is often used with smaller companies. This type of coverage would provide economic assistance for specific business expenditures, such as rent and payroll, in the event one of the owners was suddenly no longer able to work.

In addition, there are a variety of commercial insurances that should be considered, the most common being property, general liability, worker's compensation, and business interruption insurance.

It's very important that business owners work with professionals who understand the owners' specific industries, and it's critically important for an owner to have a thorough comprehension of exactly what a particular policy does and does not cover from an overall risk perspective.

Nonqualified Deferred Compensation Plans

One of the highest regarded intangible assets is the human capital that drives revenue. Buyers and sellers alike worry about employee retention.

When CEOs are asked what keeps them up at night, the most frequent answer is "people." They fret about their ability to attract top tier executives and employees. Then, once they have them, they agonize about keeping them.

When a company is sold, a buyer worries that key employees will leave, taking customers with them and provoking plummeting sales.

Competition for talent is at an all-time high and so is the price tag for losing employees. According to the Society of Human Resource Management (SHRM), direct replacement costs of an employee are as high as 50 to 60 percent of an employee's annual salary, with total costs associated with turnover ranging from 90 to 200 percent of annual salary.[13] Once a replacement is found, it may still take months of training before a full return on investment is earned.

There are many strategies to best retain employees, beginning with hiring the right people for the right positions, aligning corporate culture with employee values, investing in employee professional development, and offering fringe benefits superior to your competition. Health insurance, compensatory time off, retirement savings plans, and life insurance are all key benefit packages that keep employees devoted to their jobs and your business.

A smaller business is always vulnerable to a larger company poaching their key employees because a larger entity often will have a more generous set of benefits.

One of the best strategies to ensure that your top talent doesn't jump ship is to offer a deferred compensation plan. A qualified deferred compensation plan allows an employee to place money in a trust separate from the business (for example, a 401(k) plan).

Another type of deferred compensation plan is a nonqualified deferred compensation plan (NQDC). This allows an employer to supplement an employee's compensation with additional pay that's placed into a tax-deferred growth account. In the event of disability, retirement or other separation, this is then paid and taxed in the future to the employee or their beneficiaries. A vesting component to the plan serves as an employee retention strategy and alleviates the fear of both business owner and buyer that a key employee will stray to work for a competitor.

There are a few intricacies to consider when setting up an NQDC plan, so Jeff Carey covers the basic points:

Chris. How effective is an NQDC in attracting and retaining employees?

Jeff. NQDC plans can be extremely beneficial for attracting and retaining key employees, especially in competitive industries or when seeking to attract or retain someone with rare or exceptional talents.

Chris. What's the basic structure of a plan?

Jeff. There are some variations, but in a traditional NQDC arrangement, you would have a legal document that outlines the plan design and basic mechanics. Typically, it would outline a program where funds can be invested on a tax-deferred basis for the benefit of participating employees. Funds can be contributed by employers, employees, or in some instances, both. Funds are generally taxed to the employee upon distribution, at which time, the employer may be eligible for a tax deduction.

A couple other key features are that participants can be individually selected by the employer without any participation mandates, vesting schedules are often used, and there are typically no funding limits, as there are with a 401(k).

Chris. Is an NQDC cost prohibitive to set up for small businesses?

Jeff. Generally, no. Customarily, the employer would simply establish a predetermined budget and a plan would be designed accordingly. The key, of course, is making sure that the commitment is meaningful enough to create the desired effect. (Typically, it's 10–30 percent of a key employee's annual salary.)

Chris. How is the benefit obligation funded?

Jeff. Plans typically use either mutual funds or insurance-based funding. Ideally, an analysis should be conducted to determine the most optimal solution.

Since the funds remain on the company balance sheet, capital gains can be a factor with traditional mutual funds. In some instances, insurance-based plans can have some tax benefits that may create more efficiency.

A proper analysis will guide you to determine which is the best option for your business.

Chris. What are the advantages to the employer?

Jeff. The employer benefits from a tax deduction when funds are distributed. In addition, by creating an economic incentive for key employees, they are persuaded to stay with the employer. This can help to create better long-term continuity and reduce the high costs associated with consistent staff turnover.

Well-designed plans can also assist in making key employees a more economically viable consideration as it relates to succession planning and exit strategy. In some instances, NQDCs may also have a positive impact in negotiating with an outside acquirer who has concerns about retaining key employees after a buyout is completed.

Chris. What are the advantages to the employee?

Jeff. The employee enjoys an overall increased economic benefit. In addition, they get the advantage of leveraging tax deferral. This reduces taxable income in the near-term and allows the invested funds to grow more efficiently than a traditionally taxed investment strategy.

When a buyer analyzes a business's attractiveness, their perception of value increases if the tangible and intangible assets are protected.

You wouldn't invest in a home without it being properly insured. You buy riders for your insurance policy to protect against the loss or damage of valuables, such as jewelry and art. Your business is no different. It's an asset that requires protection from events that may or may not be foreseeable, so you can successfully sell your business when the time is right.

TAKE ACTION

- Create contingency plans for all the potential threats you can identify for your business.
- Review your buy-sell agreement to be sure the business value and funding mechanisms are up to date.
- Review the adequacy of your business insurance.
- Consider implementing an NQDC plan with a vesting component for your key employees.

MASTER EXIT PLAN
STEP IV

*Recognize When
It's Time to Exit*

Chapter 9

Do You Sell or Do You Grow?

ONCE YOU'VE ESTABLISHED your business, personal and financial objectives and understand your business's value, you can now make an informed decision as to whether you can indeed meet your goals by going to market now or if you should hold, continue to grow, and further reduce the risk in the business.

Let's go deeper into how the valuation will be applied to your decision to go to market.

> A CNBC business succession survey notes that 78 percent of small business owners expect to sell their business to fund anywhere from 60 to 100 percent of their retirement.[14]

If there's a gap between your financial goals and your business's value combined with your other financial resources, then you may decide to institute changes to increase the transferable value of your business. This will optimize and increase the value in preparation to go to market at a future date. Most of our clients choose to create a Master Exit Plan years in advance of their exit to ensure the business is well positioned to sell in the future.

If your decision is to go to market now, despite a gap in financial resources, you will need to adjust your retirement goals to match the available liquidity to fund the next stage in your life.

Calculate the Opportunity Cost of Business Ownership

Understanding the opportunity cost and risks of owning your business can also serve as a guide in making the decision to go to market. Owners who've successfully sold their businesses recognized well in advance how much of their wealth was concentrated in an illiquid asset in which the return was subject to market conditions. They may believe that *selling* their business could never provide as much financial security as *owning* the business with all the perks and benefits. However, that presumes all things remain the same. We call that the "paradise paradox," when in fact, statistically, many are actually paying for the privilege of working.

By selling your company and investing the proceeds in a well-diversified investment portfolio, the returns likely will surpass any benefit of running your business without the work and risk. The 20–30 percent who go to market and successfully execute a sale understand the benefit of asset diversification.

Matt grew his insurance agency from $700,000 of annual revenue to $5 million in less than five years. But, as noted, he was uncomfortable with most of his wealth being tied up in his business. This ultimately motivated him to sell and "take most of the chips off the table."

Here's an eye-opening example of an opportunity cost and paying for the privilege of working.

Selling price 10x EBITDA[15]		$25,000,000
Selling expenses	-	$1,200,000
Tax basis	-	$1,000,000
Gain on sale		**$22,800,000**
Federal and state capital gains tax (20% federal tax, 3.8% NIIT,[16] 5.2% state tax)	-	$6,612,000
Investable cash proceeds		**$16,188,000**
Average return on investments 9.2% (based on Goldman Sachs 140-year average)		$1,489,296
Federal and state capital gains investment tax	-	$431,896
Net investment income		**$1,057,400**
Salary, perks, benefits received	-	$450,000
Paying for the privilege of working		**$607,400**

Note: The structure of the deal affects the tax analysis. You must have your CPA perform an analysis based on your particular situation. The example above is for illustrative purposes only.

Ask yourself, "Is the risk of owning my business worth it versus selling and diversifying my wealth by investing the cash proceeds?"

Gauging your exit readiness is also important when making the "big decision." There are three main factors to consider.

1. Is the business positioned to be sold successfully?
2. Are you, the owner, ready financially?
3. Are you ready emotionally?

Assessing Your Personal Exit Readiness

The answers to the questions above are critical to determine whether you are ready to take your company to market today or if you need to better prepare for a future exit. Make the following assessments of your business, finances and emotions to gauge how ready you are.

Business Preparedness

1. **Is my company positioned to attract investors?**
   Most privately held business owners believe that value is solely driven by profit. While past performance and future projected cash flow are vitally important, the eight primary qualitative characteristics presented in "Chapter 6: Will Your Business Attract a Buyer?" on page 77 have a significant impact on value and the buyer's motivation to invest in your business. For example, if you have employees who are highly skilled and loyal to your company, an investor may pay a premium to purchase your business to acquire those employees. In a tight labor market, this can be a compelling motivation for buyers.

2. **Do I have a comprehensive plan to exit my company that aligns my objectives?** The sale of your company is just one aspect of the exit process. Remember, an appropriate plan integrates your business, personal and financial objectives. This will ensure you won't regret any of your decisions and that, upon exit, you can go on to your next chapter financially secure and continuing to lead a fulfilling life.

Financial Preparedness

3. **Have I had a mergers and acquisitions business valuation completed to understand the market value of my company?** The majority of a privately held business owner's wealth is tied up in their company. Understanding the potential selling price of your business after taxes and liabilities and then integrating the possible investable proceeds into your personal financial planning will inform you if your objectives can be met upon exit.

   As discussed in "Chapter 7: What's Your Business Worth?" on page 89, there is no magic formula for valuing a business. A third-party sale is complex and requires a quantitative and qualitative analysis performed by an exit planning advisor who specializes in M&A. The ultimate value of your company will always be driven by the quality of the team that leads the process and brings the buyers to the table, and the economic timing of your deal.

4. **Do I know when the right time is to sell my business?** Timing is a critical component of successfully exiting your business and is dependent on the marketability of your business, industry conditions and the economic cycle. It is imperative that you assess the economic factors fueling capital availability and buyer activity, which we will explore in greater detail in the next chapter.

Emotional Preparedness

5. **Am I ready for my life after the sale of my company?** A post-ownership plan will ensure that when you sell your business and enter the next phase of your life, you have addressed the

intellectual, physical and social changes as you transition. It is vitally important you prepare in advance for this next step. You may have operated your business for years, even decades, so transitioning from your business must be well-strategized to ensure you are satisfied after the sale.

Your vision for your future will serve as a guide while an exit strategy is identified. For example, you may want to continue consulting for the new owner and need a long-term employment contract negotiated or you may be ready to ride off into the sunset to enjoy a full retirement. Or perhaps you would like to participate in the growth of the company under the new ownership and want to roll equity into the new entity under a recapitalization structure.

The exit strategy that is right for you will be highly dependent on your business and financial objectives. Whatever your desired intended future is, it will require pre-planning to ensure your continued personal fulfillment after you sell your company.

In addressing these critical questions, we at Legacy Partners can guide an owner to understand if the timing is right to take their business to market and identify the exit strategy that will meet their goals.

Business owners, however, often struggle to find a balance between their personal needs and the demands of their primary stakeholders, which includes their employees and family.

Patrick started his manufacturing business in consumer products thirty years ago. "Without my employees, I never would have achieved this level of success," he explained. He felt a debt of gratitude toward his employees and thought perhaps his strategy should be to sell the company to his management team.

To compound his confusion, he also had a son working in the business who had gone to school to become a packaging engineer and had dedicated over ten years to working for him. Patrick felt equally compelled to hand his legacy down to his son and exit through a family succession. "After all, my son did go to school to work in the family business," he reasoned.

Even though Patrick had some ideas of how he wanted to exit his business, nevertheless, there were several additional considerations that needed to be evaluated to ensure that the chosen strategy, when executed, was successful. As we walked him through the process of identifying which exit strategy would best align with his goals, he realized that his management team, while exceptional in their individual roles, collectively lacked the ability to continue to grow the company without him as their leader. His son, while a very talented packaging engineer, lacked the leadership skills to take over the helm and successfully run and grow the company.

There were other factors that Patrick needed to address, beyond his desire to reward his team. For example, his emotional and financial readiness.

Patrick was surprised at the different exit strategies that were available. "I consider our business to be creative, but I had no idea of the various ways an exit strategy can be structured to meet my needs," he remarked as we led him through the process.

Recognizing that he was emotionally ready to retire and was also in a financial position to do so, his primary concern was focused on rewarding his key employees. We advised that the optimal strategy to meet his goals would be to sell to a financial buyer who would recognize the value of his employees and continue to rely on their talents.

A financial buyer, unlike a strategic buyer, doesn't want to run the company day-to-day. Instead, they bring capital and expertise to the table, and rely on current management and staff to grow the enterprise under their direction.

Patrick's deal was therefore structured as a recapitalization with a 20 percent equity roll, which he then used to reward his key management team, including his son.

Patrick was emotionally and financially ready to exit and was able to meet his business and personal goals by selling to a financial buyer.

Identifying the right exit strategy for you will depend upon your unique situation and your business, financial and emotional preparedness. To assess your readiness, we have a quiz on our website that will be helpful in guiding you. You can find it at legacypartnersllp.com/quiz.

In the next chapter, we'll explore timing considerations for the execution of your plan as you make your big decision.

TAKE ACTION

- Based on your business valuation (minus estimated expenses and taxes), calculate the financial opportunity cost of owning your business.
- Consider your tolerance for risk at your current stage in life.
- Identify which of the four types of business owner you are and which potential exit strategy would meet your goals.

Chapter 10

What's Your Timing?

Now that you know the professionals you need on your team to execute the sale of your business successfully, let's talk about when to sell. There are good times and there are bad times to sell a business. Every industry is different, and even when it's considered a bad time to sell, there are always going to be great companies that do. However, you need to know what factors influence the amount of capital available to buy businesses, which in turn drives deal volume.

I'm often asked, "Does it really matter when I sell my company?" My answer is a resounding, "Yes!"

How well-positioned your company is in the eyes of a buyer matters. How much capital is available in the market to buy businesses also matters.

The right time to sell a business is when two things are true:

1. You've built a great business with transferable value and future growth potential.
2. The market timing is right for you and your industry.

If you meet those two criteria, sell. Run your business as if you will run it forever, but be prepared to sell it tomorrow by understanding the value of your business and the significance of market conditions. If you wait until you have an offer on the table and are caught off guard, the outcome will most likely mirror that of the majority of business owners who go to market and never complete a deal.

The timing to sell your business can make a big difference in the ROI you receive for all the hard work you invested in building your company. If you've always thought you would sell your business when you're ready to retire, and we end up in an economic contraction when you turn sixty-five, that's bad timing. The optimal time to sell a company is when your business has value illustrated with a strong future financial projection that an investor sees as attractive and buyers are motivated by economic conditions.

It's often said that timing is everything. Successful people are accused of being lucky because of it. But those who work harder are always luckier, and those who are prepared in advance to execute their exit strategy when conditions are driving premiums are lucky too!

In the M&A industry, you will hear, "If you have a great business with a strong trajectory of growth, the business will sell." Yes, this is true, but don't believe that the economy won't affect the final price paid. For example, middle-market deal terms often include an earn-out. So, if the benchmark is tied in any way to economic performance, such as sales, and the economy is retracting, you might never realize that earn-out.

If you sell to a financial buyer and receive equity in the new entity at close, the future economy will certainly affect the value of that equity position. If, however, you sell with a bright long-term economic forecast and the prospect of realizing future growth is stellar, your deal terms will be less risky.

Recessions are always bad for deals. Big corporate mergers are not as affected by economic fluctuations, but I can assure you the middle market always feels the burn when interest rates increase and capital dries up.

Another scenario in which timing is critical involves a big strategic buyer who's in the process of consolidating an industry by swallowing up the small players. In that situation, you certainly don't want to be the last in line.

So how do you know if the timing's right?

Recognize the Economic Indicators

There are internal and external factors that influence a business's market readiness. We addressed the internal factors previously, with the analysis of the eight pillars that drive transferable value, all of which you have 100 percent control over. The valuation process determines whether you developed a business with transferable value, have potential for future growth, and are well positioned to go to market.

Don't make the mistake of waiting to sell because you're waiting for your business to be at its "peak." Always remember that a buyer is looking for future growth potential, so the timing is right to sell your business when there's a strong upward trajectory of potential growth.

External factors dictate the amount of capital available—and thus buyer activity in the M&A market—and you don't control any of these factors. Buyers are motivated to invest in companies if they believe they can get their required return on investment, which is primarily influenced by economic conditions, geopolitical factors, and industry health.

Just like economic cycles, we have cycles in M&A. The economy leads, and the M&A cycle lags behind. When the economy is healthy, we see premiums paid for companies, and conversely, when the economy is destabilized, prices for companies retract.

The three "Big C's" that influence investor behavior are cash, credit and confidence. Let's take a closer look at each of them.

Cash

The availability of capital drives deals, and fiscal policy affects the availability of cash for investors. For example, The Tax Cut and Jobs Act enacted in 2017 reduced the corporate tax rate to 21 percent for many companies, which had the impact of increasing cash reserves used for stock buybacks and M&A deals. Due to the increased free cash flow, valuations soared, which meant stock value climbed.

Corporate buyers use stock shares as currency in deals, so the higher the price, the higher the deal value. It's common for a public acquirer to use a stock swap transaction structure, especially when the owner of the business being acquired is staying on.

When cash is plentiful, corporations lean on growing through an acquisition strategy. As Peter Drucker would say, "It is faster, easier and cheaper to grow through acquisitions than it is to grow organically."

As of 2020, private equity has raised historic levels of uncommitted cash, also known as "dry powder," as investors look for better returns than can be achieved in the public markets. Whether a strategic or a financial investor, if there's capital available, they will always be searching for good companies to invest in. So, pay attention to cash availability when assessing if it's a good time to enter the market.

Also, a shift in fiscal policy, like capital gains tax rates, will affect seller activity. Federal capital gains tax is the first big bite out of a seller's deal, so paying attention to what the tax rate is today and projecting into the future is important when assessing the timing to bring your business to market.

Looking back at the history of the capital gains tax, we had a rate close to 40 percent in the late 1970s in the United

States, while the top ordinary income tax rate at that time was 70 percent. We've also had a capital gains rate as low as 15 percent thanks to President George W. Bush. Every administration ponders the capital gains rate, and there is nowhere for the rate to go but up from the Bush era.

On a $5 million deal at the 2022 capital gains tax rate, the federal government would receive $1 million in capital gains tax. (Note that I'm leaving out the 3.8 percent net investment income tax that's often layered on top of the federal capital gains tax.) If the capital gains tax were to double to 40 percent, your obligation to the IRS would inflate to $2 million.

Proper timing includes understanding where tax policy is today and where it's going. This also underscores the importance of having the right team members who are invested in doing everything they can to help you reduce your tax obligation.

Credit

Standard monetary policy moves interest rates. If our economy becomes overheated and there's concern for rising inflation, the Federal Reserve will raise interest rates to chill the expansion. Conversely, if our economy is sputtering, the Federal Reserve will lower interest rates to encourage lending, which promotes investment and spending, thereby stimulating the economy. The level of consumer spending will always be the main indicator of the state of our economy. Traditionally, when interest rates and the cost of capital are low, we have a higher velocity (or flow) of money, which promotes a healthy economy. As a result, buyers are motivated to invest in businesses.

Recently, it has been noted globally that lowering interest rates has not been an effective policy in stimulating economies; therefore, quantitative easing was introduced. This is an unconventional monetary policy in which central banks buy government bonds and other financial assets to inject liquidity into their banking system. Basically, they print money out of thin air.

This policy was originally introduced in the United States during the 2008 financial crisis when the Federal Reserve and central banks around the world stabilized their banking systems to avert a collapsing global economy.

However, this policy of printing money results in the devaluation of our fiat currency, which ultimately leads to inflation. Then, to control inflation, interest rates are raised.

There have also been discussions to institute a negative interest rate policy if quantitative easing isn't effective in stimulating the economy. Yes, the Federal Reserve could, in essence, charge you rent for parking your money in a savings account. Parts of Europe and Japan have instituted negative rate policies in the past to counter deflationary concerns and encourage bank lending, consumer spending, and investment.

This policy is akin to a Hail Mary pass as a last resort, and it punishes savers. If you're retired and living on interest-bearing accounts, this policy will erode your funds and jeopardize the success of your retirement plan.

Debt financing is the most common way to finance a deal. If interest rates are low, then buyers can afford to pay more for your business. You could use the same thought process in thinking about buying a home. And again, I don't mean to compare buying a home with buying a business, as these are two very distinct assets. But the rationale is the same.

It all comes down to principal and interest. The lower your interest rate, the more you can afford to borrow toward principal, which allows you to buy a bigger house. The lower the debt burden, the more a buyer can pay to invest in your company.

If you're assessing whether it is a good time to sell a business, watch interest rates. Historically, if we see inverted yields, meaning long-term debt instruments, like the ten-year treasury, are paying lower yields than short-term instruments, like the two-year treasury, then a recession is impending.

An inverted yield curve tends to precede a recession by twelve to eighteen months. This has accurately predicted every recession since 1955, with one exception in the 1970s, when we experienced an economic pullback that wasn't quite a recession.

When the economy contracts, capital goes with it and indicates a downward shift in the M&A world. So, you want to sell when interest rates are low, capital is available, and your business value is high. Low rates indicate a good time to sell, but watch for inversions.

> *Interest rates are to asset prices what gravity is to the apple. When there are low interest rates, there is a very low gravitational pull on asset price.*
>
> —Warren Buffett

Confidence

Economic confidence drives investor behavior, and it seems this can, at times, feel like shifting sand. Economic cycles and bubbles have been recorded as far back as the 1637 Dutch Tulip Mania, when investors speculated on the value of tulips until an ultimate crash. Our economy will always expand, peak, retract, trough and then do it again. We've recently been through the 2001 internet speculation Dot-com bubble, the 2008 housing financial crisis, and now we have an impending debt bubble.

When confidence is high, this indicates a seller's market in the M&A cycle and premiums are paid for businesses. Conversely, low confidence moves the cycle into a buyer's market and discounts are given. Movement in cycles isn't controlled by investors or sellers but is the result of dynamics in our economy, the geopolitical landscape, and the health of your industry.

The United States economy currently has unprecedented debt levels. In the third quarter of 2021, our government debt was at a staggering 122.5 percent of gross domestic product (GDP),[17] and the debt service required on this will ensure a continuation of this ballooning bubble.[18] By contrast, the government debt to GDP ratio during the Great Depression was 16 percent.[19]

Corporate debt has been fueled by years of low interest rates, and the loans are covenant-light, increasing the default risk and potential bankruptcies.

Personal balance sheets are no better with consumer debt at historic high levels for every demographic, from baby boomers to millennials. Mortgage debt, student loan debt, credit card debt, and auto debt are the source of our sins—in that order from highest to lowest.

Aging demographics also play into our economic confidence. The 2020 census estimates we have 76 million baby boomers,[20] and of those, 12 million own privately held businesses. These baby boomers were born between 1946 and 1964 and have begun to retire. That means they're selling their businesses. Not only will this demographic pour fuel on our federal spending for health care, but the statistics also present a potential imbalance between the number of buyers and sellers.

If there are more businesses coming to market than buyers and capital available to invest in these businesses, the M&A market will be thrown into a buyer's market. It all comes down to the balance between buyers and sellers—the basic economic function of supply and demand.

Geopolitical factors are unpredictable and influence our confidence due to the global shifts in political stability, trade, laws, labor, technology, population, and so on. There are many examples of geopolitical events eroding economic confidence, from the smallest events, like the 2015 Swiss franc soaring in value when the banking system untethered the value from the euro, to trade wars, resulting in tariffs being imposed supporting our economic isolationist policies, to global pandemics. Geopolitical threats are numerous, and our global economy is turbulent. External dynamics that we cannot control will always be part of the equation in determining how much confidence we have.

The health of an industry also drives buyer confidence to invest in specific business sectors. During the COVID-19 pandemic, we saw sectors like retail, entertainment and tourism decimated. We also witnessed the appreciation in value for essential businesses as they became more valuable to investors.

Industry disruption is a risk for almost every business at any time, so never become complacent. Instead, strive for continuous innovation to ensure that when you are ready to go to market, buyers will have confidence in their investment.

Investors will always continue to acquire middle-market businesses to improve earnings, enter new markets rapidly, expand their geographic reach, or acquire new technology and talent. If you've developed a strong business with transferable value and have strong projections for growth, buyers will feel confident enough to make an offer and it will be the right time for you to go to market.

———————————

Gauging market timing will always depend on the health of the economy, your industry and, specifically, your business. Be sure your company is ready to go to market at a moment's notice when capital is available, the cost of credit is low, and confidence is high.

Personal timing can get in the way too.

Another client of ours, Nick, had a well-positioned company. Suitors were calling because the business had all the characteristics a buyer wants: a strong financial forecast, a well-diversified client base, and a strong management team.

A PEG was in hot pursuit because they wanted Nick's leadership skills to run the platform into which they were rolling up companies. The deal would have been structured as a recapitalization, with Nick retaining a 20 percent equity position. Also, the economic forecast was bright, which would likely fuel future growth in value. At the same time, however, Nick was consumed with a family issue and decided to wait to go to market.

Is there a risk in waiting to go to market? Yes. Our global economy is dynamic and can turn on a dime. If inflation ramps up because of all the stimuli in our economy, interest rates will go up, the availability of capital will dampen, and deal volume will retract. If there's another pandemic and your bottom line is affected, the value of your business will take a hit as well.

You can't control everything. Nevertheless, you need to be aware of the economic forces and personal factors that may influence your success when going to market.

Timing matters, and it always goes back to the three Big C's (cash, credit and confidence), and their alignment with your own personal timing. Owners who are ready to go to market when the timing is right benefit by receiving the highest ROI possible.

TAKE ACTION

- Based on your business and industry, assess whether the timing is right to sell.
- Consider the M&A market cycle and capital availability to determine whether economic factors are favorable to sell your business.
- If your business is marketable and the M&A cycle is strong, don't delay. Go to market.

MASTER EXIT PLAN
STEP V

*Understand the Steps
to Sell Your Business*

Chapter 11

Who Will Be Your Suitor?

SELLING YOUR BUSINESS is not as simple as coming up with a price that will make you happy, advertising to find a buyer, presenting the financial statements and tax returns to support your price, negotiating a bit, and then closing the deal.

Now that you understand who it is that can help you exit your business and how to identify when the time is right, it's time to start thinking about who you might sell your business to and how you're going to find and connect with them. That's where we start with the seven steps in selling your business: engaging your deal team and creating a buyer pool.

This step of the Master Exit Plan details the execution of your sale and each stage of the process. We'll also demonstrate some of the complexities by using Dawna's case study as an example.

Dawna Mauldin and her husband Sid started SWM International, a welding shop, in 1979. They hired their first employee in 1981, which marked the beginning of a slow, but steady, growth trajectory. Over the next twenty-plus years, with a vision to become a manufacturer and position themselves as an acquisition target, they invested in computerized numerical control (CNC) machinery to service the oil and gas industry.

Initially, they supplied crossover subs—mechanical parts that are used to connect threaded components. I know this doesn't sound like a very glamorous business, but the company continued to expand by riding the crest of innovation in their industry and capitalizing on the oil shale boom. They set themselves apart from their competition by embracing cutting-edge technology, investing in their own fleet to control deliveries, and patenting their perforating guns and sub-products.

Over the course of thirty-five years, their strategy resulted in SWM growing into a 330,000 square-foot facility with over 100 employees producing $65 million in annual revenue.

Sadly, in 2015, Dawna lost Sid to cancer. She was immediately pursued by buyers but brushed them aside as she felt they were attempting to take advantage of her grief. The shale bust at the time had devalued the business, and so, for personal and economic reasons, Dawna recognized it was not the right time to go to market.

She continued to grow the company, and in 2018, having recovered revenue to its previous levels, she decided it was time to take SWM to market.

Dawna received six offers. The final deal was $45 million with a 45 percent equity roll. She was also retained as CEO with a two-year employment contract.

There are a lot of points in Dawna's case study to explore and we'll get to them, but before going knee-deep into that, let's talk about attitude and distractions. Please, when you're going to market, don't be distracted. We need you to continue with your nose to the grindstone, focusing on growing and managing the business.

Remember, a buyer is focused on their future return on investment, so we need your future projections to be as high as possible. No slacking off under the belief that you're going to be a multimillionaire at any moment. Until your deal is done, anything's possible. Dawna's deal, like many, had a curveball thrown in. If you take your eye off the ball and your financials sink, there's a distinct possibility that your deal will not consummate, or at the very least, it will be traded downward.

Let your advisor do the heavy lifting by staying focused on the deal, while you keep running and growing your business. There's nothing worse than updated financials coming in with a contraction because the owner's head wasn't in the game.

Engage Your Deal Team

At Legacy Partners, we align our clients with the right M&A team, and we know who the active buyers are and how to drive successful deals. Dawna's team was heavily involved in her industry and was aware of all the buyers who were in play.

To begin the M&A process, you can expect an engagement agreement that will outline the scope and duties of your advisors in marketing your business and executing a deal to completion. The engagement agreement will most likely include an exclusiv ity clause that gives the M&A team the exclusive right to represent your company in a sale process for a specified period. The agreement will also outline the fee structure that will determine how the M&A firm will be compensated.

The Lehman Formula is the most common payment structure, which is a sliding scale percentage based on the final sale price for the business. The higher the price, the lower the fee. The fee is often referred to as a "success fee" since it's only paid upon the successful completion of a deal.

You may have heard of a "breakup" or "termination fee" imposed upon a seller to make a buyer whole for the time and resources used to get a deal done in the event the seller backs out. Note that this buyer protection provision is found mostly in large public deals and is very uncommon in the middle market.

Once you've selected a firm to represent you in the transaction, an NDA will be executed to acknowledge a confidential relationship between your deal team and yourself. This will protect sensitive information regarding your business from being exposed to outsiders.

Create a Buyer Pool

With great marketing, you improve your odds of attracting quality investors, and it all begins with your team identifying the buyer pool.

The most common mistake a business owner makes is to believe that there's only one buyer who would be interested in their business, and often they think it's a direct competitor.

The goal of a proper M&A process is to market to a pool of buyers and entice them to enter into a limited auction. This practice is intended to create a bidding war that leads to the best deal for a seller.

As mentioned previously, there's a pace to divulging information as you go through the process. A good deal team will negotiate with multiple buyers and keep the momentum going, leading you through every gate.

Who Are the Third-Party Buyers?

Not every buyer has the same motivations or comes to the table with the same opportunities for you. We'll be looking at three different types of third-party buyers: financial, strategic and individual.

Financial buyers

The first type of buyer is a financial buyer. These investors are looking for a return on their investment via cash flow and a future exit for their holding. PEGs and family offices are the most common financial buyers in the middle market. These buyers actively pursue well-positioned businesses in which they can invest capital and expertise to grow value through increased cash flow and margin improvement. They'll often bolt smaller companies onto a larger platform or entity with the goal of doubling, tripling or even quadrupling the size of the group, and then either sell the company down the road to a larger financial investor or take it public.

Buyers of this type are primarily looking at how consistent your earnings have been and the anticipated future growth potential. They typically are not eager to invest a great deal of capital to realize future earnings or to run your business themselves. Thus, they'll rely heavily on your employees (and perhaps you in an ongoing management or consulting role) to drive the ROI they're seeking. If you're concerned about preserving your employees' jobs or you want to continue working for a few more years, this is an ideal buyer to meet those goals.

Also, if you've built your business to the highest level possible and still see future growth opportunities but lack the expertise or capital to fund the growth, a financial buyer can provide the resources needed to realize your business's optimal potential.

The deal may also be structured as a recapitalization in which the seller rolls equity into the new entity at the close. So, instead of cashing out 100 percent, the owner buys back an equity position at close, keeping them invested in the future success of their former company. This benefits the buyer and the seller with another liquidity opportunity when the new entity sells in the future—the proverbial "second bite of the apple." It should be a win-win for both sides of the deal.

Dawna's SWM International deal was structured as a recapitalization. A PEG purchased 55 percent of her company. Capital was not the primary concern to fuel growth. She needed expertise to capture more market share. The

PEG brought in a sophisticated team of engineers to support R&D and a high-level CFO to ensure they had a proper financial plan. In recognition of her strong customer ties, the PEG kept her in the role of CEO.

Dawna's primary concern in selling was that her employees be taken care of, and with her remaining as CEO, the transition of partial ownership to the PEG was seamless, with no impact on employees. She was also not emotionally ready to retire, so continuing to work with an opportunity for a minimum potential 3x return on her 45 percent equity position was appealing. The PEG's current goal is to sell in three years.

Another positive Dawna cited was that ownership of a private business can be very lonely—as an owner, you're top dog with nobody to bounce ideas off. She's enjoyed working and collaborating with a sophisticated and expanded team as they continue to grow the company together.

I don't mean to imply, however, that a recapitalization is without risk. There are always risks in every business transaction, and we guide our clients through the process of determining what percentage of equity they would like to roll by understanding the risk factors, such as any debt load, to facilitate the original deal. By rule of thumb, the greater the leverage or debt in the deal, the greater the equity stake the seller has in the next transaction because they're taking on risk.

For example, let's say two equal partners sell their business with an enterprise value of $20 million and buy back a 20 percent post-closing rollover equity position worth $4 million. Their equity position in any future sale will be 40 percent if the deal was funded with $10 million of debt. So, if the PEG then sells the business for $80 million after several years, the original seller receives a return of $32 million on an original $4 million equity investment. Not bad. It's common for the second liquidity event to be greater than the original transaction for a seller.

There's been much discussion about PEGs since highly leveraged deals—like Toys R Us—first came into the spotlight back in 2017. There are two different types of PEGs that rule the roost: efficiency and growth. Efficiency PEGs focus on running the organization lean to boost the bottom line as quickly as possible. Growth PEGs operate more like strategic buyers in that their strategy is to grow by bolting companies onto a platform to achieve economies of scale and improved margins. Therefore, if your buyer pool includes a PEG, it's important to evaluate risk by understanding their motivation and how much leverage will be used to grow the platform.

Strategic buyers

Another type of buyer is a strategic buyer. They seek businesses that offer a synergistic fit to their existing operations, making the whole greater than the sum of the parts. I always describe synergy as one plus one equals three. These buyers run in the same race as you. They're your larger competitors, customers or vendors. They're motivated by the opportunity to either expand quickly into new geographic regions or product lines. They may be searching for customer expansion or supply chain depth. Perhaps they need to shore up a weakness in one of their core functions (for example, in technology or distribution). It always comes down to the basics—the opportunity for cost savings, increased revenue, market expansion, economies of scale, or diversification resulting in a reduction of risk.

These buyers are long-term investors and pay high premiums for strong synergies. Because the free cash flow is adjusted for cost efficiencies as a result of this synergistic fit, the valuations are often higher than a financial buyer. Cost savings are often gained by eliminating any duplication in roles, so if your goal is to save every employee's job, a strategic buyer may not be right for you.

> **Matt**, from our first chapter, purposely positioned his company to attract a strategic buyer within his industry who would value his expertise in risk management through alternative funding. At the time of his exit, he'd exhausted his capacity to service additional clients, so he was interested in a buyer who could provide resources—specifically human capital—to grow the company while allowing him to maintain his independence.
>
> His targeted auction included eight strategic buyers, which were eventually narrowed to three. Matt's unique value proposition drove the price and terms higher than he anticipated, but at the end of the day, he made his choice based on the personalities and the degree of autonomy he would be afforded during his earn-out period, not price.

Individual investors

The third type of buyer you may encounter is an individual investor. They may be wealthy individuals searching to invest in a business or people who have left the corporate world and now aim to try their hand at owning a business. Often they'll say that they want to "control their own schedule." Don't tell them that as a business owner, it will be the customers and employees who will dictate their life! Ah, the dream that entrepreneurship means more control. What a nice, cozy delusion. They do, however, have specific expertise from their years of corporate experience. Perhaps they were in a marketing department, the head of finance or human resources, or they specialized in operations or technology. Typically, they'll be related to your industry in some capacity.

Such investors will rely on your team without hesitation, and they'll be geographically sensitive, so there usually won't be any concern about them moving the business or eliminating employees. They may or may not have access to capital, so the terms for payment will be important. The biggest question is whether they have the capabilities needed to run your business. You don't want to accept a note as payment and have the business fail because the new owner didn't have the skills to be successful.

How and to whom you market your business will make a big difference in your success. It isn't just about providing financial statements and tax returns to a potential buyer. The quality of your documentation and ability to execute your marketing strategy will ultimately drive your process. But first things first. You need a pool of buyers.

It's often said in the M&A world that "one buyer is no buyer." While it may be true that all we need is a single buyer to consummate a deal, to get the best terms and potentially the highest price, it's best to engage with multiple buyers in what's called a "limited auction."

There are degrees as to how big an auction will be. If your business is less than $1 million in revenue, you or a business broker may choose to list on the open market. Above the $1 million mark, your advisor may host a more strategic, targeted auction where they understand who the active buyers are in your sector.

Confidentiality is critical, and typically a cap will be imposed on the number of buyers invited to the targeted auction—perhaps ten or so. Any more will do little to improve the odds of obtaining offers.

In other situations, it may make sense to hold a limited or broad auction instead. A limited auction may have up to fifty buyers, and a broad auction may have one hundred or more buyers in your pool. Maintaining confidentiality is a consideration when determining what size auction you want. The larger the pool, the greater the risk of breaching confidentiality, whether deliberately or inadvertently. Also, be aware that buyers may back out if they believe you're just trying to drive the price above market.

Recognize that beauty is always in the eye of the beholder. Whether a financial, strategic or individual investor, all will have their own vision for the future, and that's why your buyer pool should be diverse. I've been surprised more than once by who ended up buying a client.

We like to see the three buyer "Big C's" in your pool: capital, competition and commitment. You need buyers who are vetted and have the capital to invest in your business. Competition among buyers ensures that the best possible terms can be achieved to reach your goals. Committed parties are motivated to engage in the process properly.

When developing a buyer pool, we collaborate with our clients to identify all possible candidates. Often our clients have previously been approached by a buyer, and we'll add them to the list. Your advisor will be aware of the investors who are active in your sector. Through this process of identification, a buyer list is created, and then you'll move on to marketing.

TAKE ACTION

- Put on your thinking cap and identify all
  potential buyers for your company. Who has
  reached out to you directly or indirectly,
  expressing interest in your business over the
  years? Who have you engaged with in your
  industry that would prove to be a synergistic
  buyer? Refer all names to your advisor, who will
  begin to formulate your buyer pool and start
  the marketing process.

Chapter 12

How Will You Capture a Buyer's Attention?

TYPICALLY, the longest part of the sales process is marketing. Once it is determined that your business is indeed marketable based on the quantitative and qualitative analyses, the odds of your business selling will depend on the quality of your documentation, which needs to effectively communicate value to the buyer.

Develop Your Marketing Collateral

Your marketing documents will drive the quality of your buyer pool. The documentation must convey the exceptional characteristics of your business and lay out its future growth potential, since this is how an interested buyer will receive a return on their investment.

Enormous amounts of information and data are collected during the quantitative and qualitative analyses. This isn't only to determine the value of your company, but also to create the marketing documents that will attract buyers.

The confidential business profile (CBP), sometimes referred to as an "executive summary" or "teaser," is the first marketing document that is sent to your pool of buyers. It's a one-page, high-level overview of your business, and like any marketing collateral, this needs to be created with an economy of words to impart the attractiveness of your company to a buyer in a compelling fashion.

Should a financial person or a marketing person write your CBP? A marketing person with a finance background is the way to go. Investors receive thousands of these per year and yours needs to stand out quickly to capture their attention. It takes about five seconds for a potential buyer to make the decision to pass or dive in deeper.

So, what's in a CBP? It's confidential, so the name of your business isn't disclosed. But it will provide an overview of your business, industry and perhaps the geographic location. The focus of this document should be on your company's growth potential, and the document needs to include financial information about past performance as well as future financial projections. The CBP should also outline all the company's unique qualities that will be enticing to a buyer, such as depth of management team, customer base, recurring revenue characteristics, and other intangible assets.

The objective of the CBP is to drive interested buyers toward signing an NDA and requesting a confidential information memorandum (CIM).

A unilateral NDA is executed to protect the seller from having any sensitive information, such as financial or trade secrets, from being shared outside the confidential relationship. Typically, the NDA is created by the seller and provided to the buyer for signature. If a business owner is contacted directly by a buyer looking for a proprietary deal, the buyer may offer the owner their NDA. Be wary of what you sign.

Prior to becoming a Legacy Partners client, Paul was approached directly by a strategic buyer who offered him their NDA. Not having access to a good advisor, Paul signed the document, which included a clause indicating that the buyer would not be prohibited from hiring employees from the company prior to consummating the deal.

The transaction was never completed, and the buyer then attempted to hire one of Paul's key executives.

If you have representation, they will send a standard NDA to all vetted buyers that protects you. If you don't have representation and you're presented with a buyer's NDA, you absolutely must have it reviewed by an attorney.

There's a case study in which a PEG pursued eighty companies, signed no NDAs, bought two of the targets, and then pursued the top talent of the other seventy-eight companies to help fuel their growth.

Anybody you're sharing confidential information with must sign an NDA that's provided by your team. No exceptions!

Commit to the process and never risk voiding confidentiality.

When you go to market, maintaining confidentiality for as long as possible is critical. If the fact that you're selling your business is prematurely disclosed to your competitors, customers, suppliers or employees, it can gouge the value of your business.

If confidentiality is voided, trust is threatened. Competitors may try to steal customers, and customers may welcome a new vendor if they're fearful that their supply chain may be disrupted. Suppliers could potentially become fearful that payments may get caught in a transition of ownership and could renegotiate terms. Thirty-day payment terms may shift to "due upon receipt," causing a cash flow crunch. Employees, one of the most highly valued intangible assets, may panic and proactively search for a new job or be poached by competitors.

Selling your business is a big decision, like getting married. You don't want to walk down the aisle halfway, then bolt. It will cost you dearly, and I'm not talking about catering expenses. Sometimes an owner is curious as to the price the market will bear. But this isn't a situation where you can say "yes" to a proposal and back out with no repercussions. Never go to market because you're curious about the price you might command. You're either 100 percent in, or you opt not to go to market. The risk is too great to be straddling the middle.

A commitment to sell your business requires that you protect the confidentiality until the deal closes and funds are wired to your investment account. That means you don't tell your employees until advised to do so. It doesn't matter how much you love them. Don't tell your best friend or your mother. There is a right time and a right way to divulge this information, and your M&A advisor will be your guide as to when the time is right.

Key employees may need to be involved in discussions. Even so, a strategy to maintain confidentiality must be in place before you go to market, such as a "stay bonus," whereby the employee is rewarded for being integral to a successful sale and transition of the business to the new owner. At times, to hammer home the importance of confidentiality with a key employee, we have them sign an NDA reminding them they're legally bound to maintain confidentiality.

There may be a time during the process when your employees and other critical relationships need to be informed of an impending transfer of ownership. But let your advisor guide you as to when and how to disclose this sensitive information. Remember, the more people who unintentionally know about the potential sale of your company, the less you may be paid for it.

You are at the point in the process where you've valued your business, optimized your strengths, shored up your weaknesses, have begun the process to execute your sale, created a buyer list, and sent out the CBP. Now those investors who are interested in gaining more information and have signed an NDA will been sent the CIM.

The CIM is a marketing document that relays in-depth information about your business. It tells the story of your business—what, when, why and how it operates. It's often called the "book" and is sometimes referred to as the offering memorandum. This document will include an overview of your business that presents what makes your business model unique and also high-level information about each pillar of your organization, including facilities, operations, employees and management team, customers, suppliers, sales and marketing, information technology, and a financial analysis with projections.

At this point, a buyer will know the name of your business. However, some information may be redacted in the document (for instance, the names of your customers or key supplier relationships). You don't want to give away secrets that a buyer who doesn't end up buying your business can then use to improve their operation.

The focus is heavily weighted on the overview of the business, as that establishes the positioning as to why a buyer should be interested in investing. The document will include financial projections that detail the potential growth opportunity from which the buyer will receive their return. It's critical that the information be accurate. (Do I even need to say that?) Misrepresentation in this industry can equate to fraud.

The CIM also serves as a pre-due-diligence checklist for a buyer and gives them enough information to establish if the proposed investment meets their criteria. It's important to note that buying a business costs a buyer both time and money.

They'll invest in accounting, legal and expert analysis fees to get a deal done. So, at this point, they're assessing if investing in your business will provide the synergies they may be looking for and the ROI they require. Buyers sometimes look at thousands of books, and yours needs to stand out.

The CIM provides enough information for a potential buyer to assess the opportunity and make an initial determination of whether an investment makes sense. It's a gate in the process that will drive those buyers who are interested in pursuing a deal to issue an indication of interest (IOI).

Analyze Your Offers

An IOI is a nonbinding agreement issued in the form of a letter that communicates a buyer's interest in purchasing your business. It will provide guidance as to a price range and may outline general points of the deal. The IOI does not narrow your choice to a single buyer, but does help sellers narrow the field.

It's worth noting that not every buyer issues an IOI. Some may go directly to a letter of intent, which we'll discuss in a moment. Once you've established which IOIs are of interest to you, the next step is to schedule a visit for the buyer to meet you and potentially your management team.

Management meetings can be stressful. They're sort of like a first date. You want them to like you and believe in your business. The outcome of the meeting is either they give you an offer or they don't—they ask you for a second date or they ghost you.

You need to get it right. So here are a few insights that we use to prepare our clients and get rid of any jitters before the buyer walks through the door.

1. Know thy enemy, or in this case, potentially your Prince or Princess Charming. I mean, get inside your buyer's head. Prior to the meeting, begin the preparation process by understanding why the buyer is

potentially interested in purchasing your business. Your team will research them extensively. Attention spans are short, and you'll need to convey why your business is a good investment quickly and concisely. Understand your buyer's *why*.

2. Once you know their why, prepare your presentation from a buyer's perspective and explain your why. Why does your business do what it does? Provide a lay of the land as to why you are successful, why your customers love you, and why there's great potential for future growth with the involvement of the potential buyer.

3. Know your numbers. Think *Shark Tank* and present your future with projected numbers and supporting KPIs. Your presentation should include data to support current revenue and sustainability of future revenue with backlog, contracts, recurring revenue data, and so on. By showing the buyer their potential ROI, you're enticing them to become part of the future of your business.

4. Understand that the buyer will be assessing you and your key management team. If you end up rolling equity in the deal, they'll be working closely with you and will want to know that you're someone they can work with to drive the business to a higher level. They also want to know that the team in place is top tier, and that the culture is a good match. Your advisor will guide you in the decision to include key team members since their presence in the meeting may be critical for the buyer to gain confidence, which will be reflected in the buyer's offer.

5. Be prepared for questions. A buyer may ask what you see as the biggest risks of your business or industry. They may ask about your competitors to assess your

view of the business's position. Or they may ask what you see as the benefit of working with them. They're assessing risks, and it will be your job to address their concerns and minimize risks they see in the business. But don't lie. Be honest, because if you uncover a risk in the industry, the buyer will almost certainly have uncovered it too. Any increased risk they see will increase their ROI requirement and reduce the price they're willing to pay.

6. "Why are you selling?" This is the question that can strike fear in a seller's eyes because they know it's a loaded question. There's a right way and a wrong way to let your buyer know why you're exiting.

    Saying with exasperation, "I'm burned out and my employees are driving me crazy!" is less than ideal, especially when the human capital in your business is what drives revenue. Better to say perhaps, "I loved building my business, but I'm ready for someone to take the reins and build on what I've been able to do." Also, the buyer, whether a strategic, financial or individual investor, will want to depend on you to help them transition into ownership. You, as the owner, are an important intangible asset for the buyer. They'll want to know that you'll be willing and able to help them grow the company for a while. The time could be a designated transition period or negotiable if you sell to a financial buyer who wants you to retain an equity position. The buyer certainly doesn't want a leader who's tired and disengaged.

    Another detrimental response is, "I think we're at the top of the mountain and have made all the money we can." Entrepreneurs tend to focus on what they can do, and they want to sell when they've brought the business to its peak. Please remember that a buyer is looking for future growth potential, and they'll contribute their resources to raise the summit to a new level. If you say the business has reached its peak and there's no more runway, the buyer may just walk away. A better statement would be, "I've driven the business as high as I can with my resources. But if the business were infused with additional financial and intellectual capital, it could grow enormously." Whatever your reason for wanting to sell, turn it into a positive in the eyes of the buyer and don't unwittingly talk them out of a deal.

Your advisor will be instrumental in preparing you and your management team for this discussion.

The management meeting also presents you with an opportunity to ask the buyer questions to help you evaluate them and their intentions. A few good questions to ask are:

- What do you see as the opportunity for investment in my business?
- What do you look for in a partner?
- What do you believe is the potential for growth?

Remember to be clear and concise in delivering information about your business. Just as importantly, be astute in listening to their answers to your questions, as the purpose of the meeting is to drive the buyer to tender an offer in the form of a letter of intent and for you to evaluate the potential investor.

The LOI is an offer that outlines fundamental terms for a deal, such as:

- Price, either reflected as a hard number or sometimes presented as a formula. (For example, 5x adjusted EBITDA.)
- Deal structure, whether an asset or stock sale.

- Contingencies, such as adherence to financial projections, debt payoff, or financing confirmation.
- Net working capital target, typically defined as accounts receivable + inventory – (accounts payable + short-term liabilities + accrued expenses).
- Escrow expectation, if any.
- Deal funding and how the deal is being financed, which will help your team identify a buyer who is likely to close the deal.
- Closing expectations and any approval stipulations.
- Exclusivity period and a no-shop clause, both of which last through due diligence.
- Management post-close, which may include their requirement for a transition period from you and key management's expected roles moving forward.

Our goal for our clients is to receive several LOIs. Your deal team will then negotiate with each buyer and guide you in deciding which to sign, indicating your acceptance of exclusivity with a particular buyer. An LOI is fundamentally a nonbinding agreement, except for the no-shop clause or exclusivity period agreed upon to allow the buyer time to get through due diligence, which is binding.

In addition to the above terms reflected in your LOI, corporate culture weighs heavily on most clients as they decide which buyer is best for them. The buyer will be working with your employees, and perhaps you too, if you decide to stay on. Therefore, assessing if the buyer is a complement to your company's values is important, as it will affect the future success of the business.

> **Matt** felt that the best buyer for him would allow him to maintain his independence, resulting in faster growth, which then would increase his earn-out bonus.

> **Dawna,** who retained a 45 percent equity position, met with a third-generation strategic buyer and found their corporate culture to be oppressive, so she didn't have confidence in their ability to gain market share or take care of her employees. As a result, she rejected their offer and went with a financial buyer instead.

Corporate culture matters in addition to the basic terms of the deal. Or, as Peter Drucker is often attributed with saying:

Culture eats strategy for breakfast.

In other words, you can have the best growth strategy in the world, but if your corporate culture is negative and your employees leave, the strategy will fail. Privately held business owners understand that their employees are one of their most highly regarded intangible assets, and it is critical the new owner's culture matches what employees have become accustomed to over the years.

Marketing your business with compelling documentation will attract multiple investors into your process so you can properly evaluate which potential buyer could meet all of your goals, including who will align with your corporate culture. If the information about your company is not well communicated, your business will be passed over by buyers. You don't want to be dead in the water trying to sell your business because your marketing didn't lure them in.

Remember, attention spans tend to be quite short these days and investors are no different. Your marketing documents must command attention. More competition always leads to better results in the price and terms.

TAKE ACTION

- Your advisor will develop impactful marketing documents for you to ultimately approve. Review them from a buyer's perspective and be sure they portray your business in a compelling fashion.

- Insist on an NDA, provided by your team, from anyone with whom you share confidential information.

- Prepare for your buyers' meetings and ask questions to gain clarity on each buyer's motivation to purchase your business.

Chapter 13

Can You Get What You Want?

YOU ARE HALFWAY through the process of selling your business. Your team has identified the optimal buyers for your pool. They have created compelling marketing collateral, which drove investors into the limited auction. They hosted buyer/management meetings, after which you received multiple LOIs. Now the all-important step of negotiation begins.

Remember, the value of your business is calculated based on data. The price you will receive upon sale will be negotiated and driven by the quality of your deal team.

Negotiate Your Deal

Your exit planning advisor and M&A team will guide you through negotiations. However, if you have a business with less than $1 million EBITDA and are going to try to sell it by yourself, at the very minimum, hire a professional negotiator. It can be your attorney if they have transactional experience.

Every sale starts out amicably and with high hopes. Eventually, however, the buyer will scrutinize your business, and if you don't like what you're hearing, your emotions could push the deal off the rails. That's why it's important to have someone else on your side who is leading the negotiation and who can help you keep your reactions in check.

The following deal points will be negotiated by your team:

- Price
- Structure
- Terms

Price

One of the biggest considerations for an owner going to market is the price. We're often asked by our clients, "I'll be paid for my goodwill right?" Goodwill is simply the difference between the value of your business and what a buyer will pay at the point in time you go to market.

We understand that you've poured your sweat and tears into building your business. Therefore, with a history of ups and downs, failures and successes—and a great deal of risk—you may think you've created enormous goodwill and that your business is worth a billion dollars. I get it, but keep in mind *greed kills deals,* and the 20–30 percent who do successfully sell keep their expectations in check.

Negotiation is an art form, and a good negotiator will increase the value by leveraging competitive offers. Another tactic to enhance the offer is understanding the synergies and quantifying the benefit to the buyer better than they can. Pinpointing the financial impact will drive the price.

The trick is to understand what the buyer is trying to achieve and then prove how purchasing your business will realize their goal. Working with our clients, we establish a predetermined zone of possible agreement on price when we begin negotiations.

Structure

In addition to the price, your deal team will be negotiating other points, such as whether the deal will be an asset or a stock sale.

If your business is a partnership, sole proprietorship, or limited liability company, the structure will be an asset sale, since these entities don't have stock. If, however, your business is an S corporation or a C corporation, then the structure will be negotiated.

In an asset sale, the seller retains the legal entity, and the buyer purchases individual assets and liabilities of the business. Typically, the cash stays with the seller, and they also retain all long-term debt obligations. This is often referred to as a cash-free, debt-free transaction.

In a stock sale, a buyer purchases the seller's stock in the company and, therefore, acquires the legal entity. The assets and liabilities acquired tend to be similar to an asset sale, so any assets the buyer doesn't want are distributed prior to the sale, and if there are any liabilities that the buyer is not acquiring, they will be paid off.

When negotiating the deal structure, the focus is primarily on the tax implications and potential liabilities. A buyer most often prefers an asset sale since any future contingent liabilities (for example, from product liability, employee lawsuits, or warranty or contract issues stemming from your ownership) will remain with the seller, reducing future risk for the buyer.

Also, in an asset sale, a buyer enjoys the tax benefits of a step-up in basis of assets, which increases their depreciation deduction and therefore, after-tax cash flow.

Taxes for the seller under an asset structure tend to be higher since assets other than intangibles, like goodwill, may be taxed as ordinary income as opposed to capital gains. And if your structure is a C-Corp, you'll be subject to double taxation, which is paid at the corporate level on the transaction and then again at the personal level upon distribution of the proceeds.

There are some negatives for the buyer to consider too, such as the assignability of assets. For example, we had a client who derived much of his revenue from government contracts. The request for proposals required that all contractors submitting bids must have a minimum of fifteen years of previous experience. Under an asset sale, the "experience" stays with the legal entity, so in this case, the structure had to be a stock sale to preserve their main source of revenue.

Sellers prefer a stock sale since it reduces their future exposure to liabilities. All the proceeds are taxed at a capital gains rate, and if you're a C-Corp, it will eliminate the double taxation conundrum. It's worth noting, though, that in the closing document, called the "definitive purchase agreement," the warranties, representations and indemnifications are negotiated, and any risk may shift back to the seller.

Often a seller thinks they cannot agree to an asset sale if their entity is structured as a C-Corp because of the tax implications. However, in exchange for agreeing to an asset structure, your team will compute the tax impact and negotiate the price accordingly to compensate the seller for agreeing to the deal structure.

> If the buyer is receiving a benefit in the structure of the deal, then the seller must be compensated for whatever concession they are making to the buyer's benefit.

For example, a 338(h)(10) election, named after that section of the IRC, recharacterizes a stock sale of an S corporation to a corporate buyer as an asset sale for tax purposes, while the transaction remains treated as a stock sale for legal purposes. The buyer then has the benefit of a step-up in basis of the assets and avoids any issues regarding the assignment of assets. Meanwhile, the seller will have a higher tax burden with this election and the deal team will negotiate accordingly to ensure additional compensation for the seller agreeing to the election, which provides a tax benefit to the buyer.

As you can see, there's much to consider when weighing the options in structuring the deal. You'll need your deal team, including your exit planning advisor, M&A advisor, CPA and attorney, to assess the risks and benefits of the structure to guide you in making the best decision for you.

Terms

"You name the price, I'll set the terms," said the seller.

Terms matter. How much you sell your company for is a big deal. How much you keep in your pocket is an even bigger deal.

After closing costs, the biggest bite out of your transaction will be from the Internal Revenue Service, so mitigating taxes is very important. You'll need a CPA who has extensive M&A transaction experience. All CPAs are not created alike, and the Internal Revenue Code is dense, so understand that most CPAs specialize in specific areas. Your CPA, who's a trusted confidant, may have been great at saving you from taxes as you grew your company. But they may have little or no experience in selling a business. A CPA experienced with M&A issues will be creative in minimizing taxes and deferring gains.

A pure stock sale will be taxed at capital gains rates. You can also defer taxes if you exchange your company's stock for stock in a public company, resulting in a corporate reorganization or tax-free exchange. It really isn't tax-free but tax-deferred. Once you sell the stock, your gain will then be subject to capital gains tax.

An asset sale may trigger capital gains or ordinary income tax, depending on the allocation of the proceeds to each individual asset sold. Some assets will be taxed at a capital gains rate, but others, such as inventory and accounts receivable, which are not typically held for more than a year, are subject to ordinary income tax rates.

As you can see, there's a push-pull dynamic to negotiating the best deal, thus the need for an excellent negotiator in addition to your CPA. For example, a buyer in an asset-structured deal will want more of the purchase price allocated toward equipment to increase future depreciation in order to decrease their tax obligation. The seller on the other side will want more allocated to goodwill, which will be subject to the capital gains rate.

Here are a few thoughts on the various forms of payments:

- **Cash** is always king. The more cash up front, the less risk for the seller.

- **Secured notes** will defer taxes as the capital gain is recognized under the installment method. There are some limitations to the deferral, depending on the amount of the note. Many middle-market deals will have a note attached to the deal. However, be wary of the amount and remember you're not a bank.

  Also, ensure that the assets used to secure the note are valued correctly and are enough to secure the entire note. We like a line of credit for the amount of the note deposited in a bank of the seller's choice at closing. This serves as a form of security since a note you receive will always be subordinate to a bank loan.

- **Retained equity** in a recapitalization or partial sale structure allows you to buy back an equity position in the business at close. A recapitalization can be enormously beneficial to a seller who's excited to help grow the company and receive another bite at the apple.

- **Stock** in a public company can have an enormous upside, as public companies use stock as currency. Some private companies do too. If you accept stock as a form of payment, recognize that stock may be illiquid. If it's a public company, it will be easier to find a buyer for your stock, while a private company's stock may be worthless.

If stock is a term you accept, there most likely will be a period in which you will be restricted from selling the stock after the close of your transaction. So, keep in mind how quickly you'll need the cash in determining your comfort with stock as consideration.

- **Earn-out** is a payment that's contingent upon meeting a specified metric that's typically tied to the income statement, such as sales or earnings. It could also be tied to a nonfinancial event, such as a regulatory approval or the retention of a big customer. It's a very common payment method in an M&A transaction, often used to bridge the gap if the seller is looking for a higher price than the buyer wants to pay immediately or the buyer is concerned that the business is too owner-dependent.

A question often asked is, "Should I accept an earn-out?" It depends on how you feel about the other terms and the risk of actually receiving the earn-out. If you feel well rewarded with the other terms of the deal and you view the earn-out as icing on the cake, go ahead and accept it. Recognize, however, that after you sell your company, you may or may not be an integral part of it going forward, and therefore you may not have any impact on meeting the benchmark established to receive the earn-out. You'll also lack control over external events that could hinder meeting the standard for the earn-out.

Ultimately, the answer lies in your assessment of the risk and the tax treatment. Whether the earn-out payment is subject to capital gains or ordinary income tax will depend on whether it represents a deferred payment for purchasing the business (capital gains rate) or compensation for your continued work under an employment agreement (ordinary income rate).

Think about it carefully. Let's say your earn-out is tied to earnings and the buyer posts unanticipated expenses to the Profit & Loss (P&L) statement, driving down earnings and putting your earn-out bonus in jeopardy. If you have a deep-pocketed buyer to throw at attorneys, are you going to go to battle over how the benchmark was calculated, believing you'll win? Nah.

A word to the wise, never agree to be paid based on a benchmark over which you have no control.

- **Noncompete agreement** is a covenant to protect the buyer from you setting up another business and competing directly against the new ownership. The agreement will have a reasonable time restriction and geographical constraint. It may also identify specific consideration paid for the covenant.

  Depending on the intent of the agreement, any consideration identified as payment for the noncompete may be taxed at either ordinary income or capital gains tax rates. Regardless of whether the deal is structured as an asset sale or stock sale, it will be taxed as ordinary income. However, if it's considered a transfer of goodwill it may be treated as a capital gain.

- **Employment agreements** are for when the buyer asks you to come on board as a consultant to help transition the business to them. It may be a short- or long-term proposition.

  Your deal team will try to negotiate the contract to stipulate that you're paid for the entire contract, even if the buyer decides to terminate it early. Any employment agreement will always be taxed at ordinary income rates.

Rely on your exit planning advisors, deal team, CPA and M&A attorney to negotiate and mitigate taxes as much as possible or defer the gain. They'll ensure you keep as much in your pocket as possible when the deal closes.

Your M&A attorney will review your LOI and identify any red flags. Once you've compared apples-to-apples on your offers, you can confidently make your big decision and sign the agreement, which indicates your exclusivity to a buyer. Your LOI is the marriage proposal. We want you to receive many, but you can only accept one.

Keep in mind that although the LOI is fundamentally a nonbinding agreement, it may be hard to back off on any points agreed to in the LOI when you get to closing and signing the DPA. Now that you have signed an LOI and are officially engaged, it's time for due diligence before the marriage is consummated.

TAKE ACTION

- Work with your advisors to be sure you understand the structure and terms of all offers received.
- Integrate your deal (minus estimated taxes and expenses) into your financial plan so you have clarity on the impact the sale will have on your wealth.
- Sign your LOI and get ready for due diligence.

Chapter 14

Will Due Diligence Kill You?

M OST SELLERS needlessly fear the dreaded due diligence phase and approach it as if it will be the Spanish Inquisition. This part of the process has come a long way since I started out as a CPA. Back then, we loaded up a conference room with documentation, and the buyer would painstakingly come in and make copies for their review. It always seemed to be an endless process. Today, everything is much more efficient, and we set up your virtual data room in the cloud the minute you come on board as a client.

Due Diligence

The buyer will often hire a third-party accounting firm to perform due diligence to substantiate the accuracy and sustainability of the company's historical earnings and future cash flow projections. This analysis will be presented in a quality of earnings (QOE) report to your buyer. Their analyses will focus on verifying all financial information, the concentration of customers, growth potential, supply chain quality, employee and management depth, competitive position, durability of customer contracts, obsolete inventory, liabilities, and so on.

The due diligence review is comprehensive.[21] In addition to the accounting firm's financial review, there may be specialists who are brought in to analyze the following: property, personnel, legal, intellectual property, insurance, government, general corporate, environmental and compliance. All specialists can execute their reviews simultaneously, making the exercise very efficient and seamless. The data room is secured in the cloud with access easily granted and revoked. Depending on the complexity of your deal, you can expect about a 60-day due diligence period.

Buyers sometimes may drag their feet in completing due diligence because the longer it takes, the better the chance of the deal being renegotiated. Once you start due diligence, your leverage is diminished, so we want it to go smoothly and quickly.

During the final stages of due diligence on Dawna's deal, SWM International was served with papers alleging a patent infringement. Nothing can spook a buyer more than threatened litigation. The structure was a stock sale, so the buyer would be accepting all liability. The deal stopped for months while the attorney proved the claim to be baseless.

For Matt, the due diligence with his strategic buyer was dragging on. The buyer brought in one of the big four CPA firms, which seemed to be ticking and tying every penny and monopolizing Matt's team's time. In frustration, Matt decided to pause due diligence for three months because he was going into his busy season. When the buyer heard the seller was choosing to delay, they accelerated the process, and the deal closed quickly. This was a risky strategy, but it worked.

A major characteristic of successful deals is that they are always prepared well in advance for this critical part of the process. This is why we set up a virtual due diligence data room during the valuation phase. Not only is it important to have your "house in order," so to speak. It's also important for all information to be readily available so no time is lost. The ability to anticipate a buyer's request for data can mean life and death for a deal. If there are any delays, you risk losing a buyer's interest or them losing faith in the integrity of the information, which may also translate into a renegotiation of your deal.

There must be a timeline and process of accountability that will drive meeting the buyer's deadlines. We may need to move on to another investor if the selected buyer drops out during the due diligence process. So, time is always of the essence.

There are many events out of your control that can ruin a deal, such as an industry disruption, loss of a key customer or employee, a recession, and geopolitical events. The year 2020 will go down in history for wreaking havoc on the world economies and many deals. We had a client who was entering due diligence with an anticipated close date of the end of May 2020 when COVID-19 struck. Due diligence was delayed and pencils were put down. You cannot control unforeseen external events that can throw your deal, but you can control actions that impede a deal from moving along.

Your valuation will uncover any red flags in advance of due diligence and give you an opportunity to correct all issues that may cause a problem or delay the diligence process. The goal is to prevent any opportunity for the buyer to renegotiate the deal. Note also that an adjustment to price can go both ways. As the accountants descend on the financials, they may uncover adjustments that raise EBITDA and, with it, the selling price.

Re-trading or a write-down on the deal are renegotiations of the accepted terms and purchase price. There's fair re-trading and dishonest re-trading. If something material occurs, such as your profitability plummeting due to a pandemic, then a re-trade on the deal is legitimate. Of course, there are also unscrupulous buyers who are deceptive in their intent and try to change the deal. This is the equivalent of a bait-and-switch.

To avoid the sub-par buyers, your team will vet them to ensure you're working with the most ethical investors. It's also important that as you go through the process, you're transparent with everything that affects the business. If there are no surprises, the buyer will not be encouraged to trade down.

If you feel uneasy or the buyer begins to re-trade the deal, don't be afraid to walk away. This is one reason we want due diligence to move along as quickly as possible. If our team feels the deal is going to die, we want to re-engage with the other buyers who were part of your limited auction. Your team will keep those buyers in the wings.

The Cardinal Rule of Due Diligence:
Always disclose anything that goes wrong
to the buyer as soon as possible.

Dawna's deal was re-traded because her company served the oil and gas industry, which is always volatile, and the due diligence delay caused by the threatened patent litigation put her deal in the middle of the 2019 crash, which negatively affected her revenue. The re-trade on her deal, albeit not joyfully welcomed by Dawna, was justified.

The Close

Once you've come through due diligence, you'll begin to see light at the end of the tunnel. Your deal will be closed and memorialized with a DPA, which is binding and supersedes all previous discussions and documents, including the IOI, if received, and the LOI. Depending on the structure of the deal, the DPA will stipulate all key terms, such as closing date, consideration, required working capital at closing, and debt paid off to release liens.

The agreement will include a warranties, representations and indemnifications (WRI) section, which is the buyer and seller warranting that their representation statements are true. For example, a seller confirms compliance with government regulations and that their list of customer contracts is accurate or provides a list of any outstanding or potential lawsuits. The buyer will want this to be as comprehensive as possible, and of course, the seller wants to limit the list of warranties and representations. This part of the closing document may be extensively negotiated, and it's your attorney's job to protect you as much as possible. Indemnification clauses stipulate how a buyer will be compensated in the event of a breach of a seller's representations and warranties that results in a loss to the buyer.

Often a portion of the transaction proceeds, typically 5–15 percent, is held in an interest-bearing escrow account for a period of one or two years for any working capital adjustments and also as backing for the indemnity clause.

Increasingly, we're seeing the use of WRI insurance. This coverage not only can provide peace of mind to a seller with a clean exit, but also affords the buyer a direct claim with an insurance company, which will be much more efficient than seeking recourse from a seller. WRI insurance is something to think about when assessing future liability in your deal.

According to Jeff Carey of Vertex Planning Group:

> …the rise in popularity of WRI insurance has substantially increased over the last few years since the cost of coverage has been coming down steadily as more providers have entered the market.

He also described the coverage as:

> …policies that are used essentially to indemnify the seller (with limitations) if, by chance, they inadvertently withhold or provide inaccurate information during due diligence, and such disclosures, or lack thereof, ultimately

lead to economic loss for the buyer. Depending on the design, these coverage strategies will make the buyer whole, typically up to 10 percent of the overall transaction price.

Your M&A team will guide you to assess if an insurance policy for protection against a WRI claim is warranted.

There may also be covenants in the DPA, like a noncompete agreement, and other miscellaneous provisions, such as inventory description, dispute resolutions, and the governing state for disputes.

Finally, your deal is closed. There's a pile of documents that are signed by the seller and buyer, virtually or in person. The seller transfers ownership to the buyer. The buyer wires a bucket of funds into the seller's account. Your deal is done... Well, almost.

Depending on the complexity, some deals require an interim period between the signature and the actual close. Perhaps new permits need to be drawn by the buyer to operate the business, or maybe there's a lag in bank financing. At the final close, the money is wire transferred to the seller's wealth manager to be invested according to a design created well before the close.

There will also be post-closing financial adjustments that account for changes in value between the deal signing and the actual close. For example, the preliminary balance sheet used for signing won't be exact, and a final balance sheet will be prepared within the next thirty to ninety days. This will reconcile and adjust, or "true-up," any differences at closing for items such as working capital—the most common focus—or may include debt or cash balances. These adjustments are usually accounted for with the money held in escrow.

However, if the balance sheet used at signing is significantly different from the final balance sheet, it could cause a pre-closing renegotiation of price. A good deal team will help you avoid this type of eleventh-hour falling out of bed. This is yet another reason why choosing the right team members is so important.

In 1989, John Heap succeeded his father as owner of Colorado Lining, a geosynthetics contractor that provided custom fabrication, design-build and installation of geomembranes for containment of natural resources. Over the next twenty-five years, he grew the business to $32 million in annual revenue and 100 employees.

One day, in 2015, his wife posed the question, "Are you going to die at your desk or what?" His daughters weren't interested in taking over and he wasn't confident his employees could maximize the profitability of the company. So, he decided to go to market.

He received ten offers and signed one that was structured as a recapitalization. Unfortunately, the buyer suffered a financial blow prior to closing, and the deal fell through.

Timing is everything. As disappointing as it all seemed in the moment, ultimately John was happy the deal never made it over the finish line since the buyer eventually went bankrupt.

After a pause, John went back to market in 2016 and received an offer from Raven Industries, a public company that was a supplier of geomembrane material to Colorado Lining. A strategic buyer looking for vertical integration, their offer came in $6 million higher than the previous offer.

Looking to capitalize on revenue growth, Raven Industries was motivated to close quickly. Due diligence was performed by Deloitte and went smoothly, except for the assignment of a $10 million contract to the new owner, which took some time. It's not uncommon for some hiccup to occur as the finish line approaches.

The deal was finalized at $14 million in cash, plus a $2 million earn-out over three years that was tied to revenue growth and a reduction of overhead.

Most deal terms will require a seller to remain on board for a specified period to guide the successful transition to the new owner. This will likely be negotiated as an employment agreement or an earn-out. The former owner will then guide employees as they get used to the new ownership.

I will say that entrepreneurs—and especially business owners who've spent years or decades building their business—typically are not fond of becoming an employee, even for a limited time. That's something to think about when accepting the terms of your post-ownership transition period. I've also seen owners who've wanted to extend their employment contract beyond the transition. So don't automatically discount the idea.

In John's case, he described his earn-out phase as "painful." It's a common sentiment if a previous owner witnesses the new owner making mistakes. Yet, in the end, John was quite happy with his sale, had no regrets, and after his earn-out was completed, he went off to work on his ranch, focus on charity work, and do a little golfing and fishing.

John offers the following advice to business owners contemplating a sale:

- Make decisions based on logic, not emotion.
- Prepare years ahead and manage your business efficiently and professionally.
- Get your family in order and do not sugarcoat your intentions with family and employees.
- Build out where you want to end up.
- Understand your goals early in the process.

As an owner enters the final stage of selling their business, they often ask, "How do I break up with my employees?"

John recognized that retaining employees was key to a successful integration into the new company. He rewarded his key employees with a bonus based on a percentage of his earn-out.

The remaining employees were, in his words, "freaked out" about working for a large public company. They were incentivized with stock options, and 98 percent chose to stay.

Employees are a top worry for many business owners, so how and when the sale of the company is disclosed matters.

Key members of your management team may know about the sale in advance since they may have participated in management meetings and, therefore, understand the objectives of the transaction. You may have incentivized them with a stay bonus, recognizing that your management team is of great value to a buyer and will help through the due diligence process.

Most employees, however, will have no idea the ownership is changing, and if the information isn't communicated in a timely fashion and correctly, the shock and fear can have devastating results. The time to announce the deal to your general employees is once the deal has closed or when the closing is imminent. You don't want them to hear about it from a press release. That would be comparable to a text message breakup.

Create a detailed action plan as to when, what, where and how information will specifically be relayed. Often the buyer will play a role in:

- articulating the future goals of the business clearly.
- expressing how each employee plays a pivotal role.
- emphasizing the value the buyer brings to the table.

Communicating with empathy and excitement for the future will help alleviate any anxiety and reassure employees as to how important they are to the company's future success. The goal is to retain the happy, productive staff who helped you build the business and who are vital to creating a successful future for the new buyer.

Some owners opt to be more transparent and tell their employees that they're exploring selling the business early in the process. If you don't feel it will pose any concern regarding employee or customer retention, and it makes you feel good, this is an option. You can then deal with employee concerns along the way. But recognize the process takes time and consider whether you'll want to be answering their questions at every turn.

> At Legacy Partners, we feel the risk of voiding confidentiality and damaging the value of the business is too great and have never advised a client to go this route.

Every business owner, however, is unique, and we work with our clients to establish the point at which the transition should be disclosed and what information to relay. We also guide our clients through the process of announcing the transition to the outside world, such as to vendors, lenders and customers.

For some owners, telling the employees is hard. They often feel they're betraying the equivalent of family members who helped them build the company. Remember, it's you who has taken on the risk of ownership for years. Along the way, you've paid your employees fairly, while providing benefits and a sense of belonging and purpose. You don't owe your employees for life. You've kept your end of the bargain, and now it's time for you to exit your business when and how you wish.

Let's look at it another way. What if you asked your employees to guarantee they'd never leave by signing a lifetime employment contract? It's not happening. Right? So don't feel guilty for maintaining confidentiality and not telling your employees until the time is right. It's just part of the process.

At the close of your transaction, you're officially untethered. With your post-ownership plan in place, now's the time to live the life you desire. You're free to do whatever you want with your time and money.

In the next chapter, we'll discuss preserving your wealth.

TAKE ACTION

- It is critical for you to be transparent and responsive to all questions asked by the buyer and their team during the due diligence period. Do not delay in responding to any questions and be proactive about delivering all necessary information.

- Work with your advisor to create a plan for how and when to disclose the sale of your business to employees.

MASTER EXIT PLAN
STEP VI

Protect Your Wealth,
Family and Legacy

Chapter 15

Crossing the Finish Line

THE LAST STOP in the journey of selling your business is the wiring of funds into your account.

As business owners approach the finish line for their deal, they often ask, "What do I do with my money? Should I put it under the bed or in a coffee can buried in the yard?"

I don't know which scares a business owner more, not having an office to go to after their transition period or having to make investment decisions that will grow their wealth efficiently and preserve their legacy for future generations.

Throughout the exit process, you've worked with many professionals. After the close, their jobs are done. Now, your wealth management team members will support you moving forward.

Invest Your Proceeds

The sale of your business will most likely be the most important financial event of your life. Without a good wealth management team serving you, the risks are enormous. All clients of Legacy Partners are properly aligned with a financial planning team prior to closing, so their investment strategy is defined and the funds, once wired, are invested immediately. Your team will have an in-depth understanding of your financial goals and risk tolerance to design a plan that will grow and preserve your wealth.

Michael Heberlein, CFP®, ChSNC®, is a partner at Commonwealth Financial Group and a key strategic partner for Legacy Partners. He's an expert in guiding business owners in financial and estate planning, and he shared some key thoughts with me about the importance of having a sound investment strategy to protect your wealth.

CHRIS. Why should a business owner partner with a financial planner when they're as young as possible?

MICHAEL. The reasons are numerous. First and foremost, I think it's important for business owners to select a financial advisor who's well versed in working both with business owners and their other advisors—CPAs, attorneys and so on.

When it comes to retirement planning, there are some unique elements that come into play with business owners. Oftentimes, the business itself represents the largest asset on the personal balance sheet. This can lead to some added planning complexities, since closely held businesses are difficult to value and are often illiquid.

Compounding matters is the fact that many closely held businesses can't be sold for enough capital to replace the income that owners have been accustomed to while maintaining ownership. It's very important to understand this potential economic gap, and then institute a strategy for addressing it. Typically, this requires a two-pronged approach.

First, we need to create a savings and investment plan for efficiently leveraging the cash flow of the business by establishing an appropriate wealth accumulation strategy separate from the business.

Second, we then identify and leverage the key factors that increase the intrinsic value of the entity. Doing so will make the business itself more attractive to outside buyers, thus increasing the likelihood that the business can be sold for a higher multiple down the road.

CHRIS. When should the discussion begin on how to manage the proceeds from the sale of the company?

MICHAEL. The specific strategy for investing the proceeds from a business divestiture should be examined as early as possible. The benefit of doing so is that you can better coordinate asset location, as well as allocation. Simply put, certain assets are better off being held in certain types of accounts, but the logic can change based on prevailing tax and macro factors. If there is a large amount of nonqualified assets suddenly on the horizon, then it may be advantageous to consider making certain portfolio changes in advance.

A well-thought-out and efficient plan for creating ample amounts of income once the business is sold is very important since there will be no more traditional paychecks coming in. It is also critically important that a seller has a genuine understanding of exactly what is needed on a net basis, post-transaction, to ensure that their desired lifestyle expenditures can be met without fear of outliving their capital. This is something that should be thoroughly examined prior to entering any formal negotiations and is a key component of Legacy Partners' exit process.

CHRIS. Why is it important to coordinate the business owner's estate plan with the financial plan?

MICHAEL. When it comes to comprehensive wealth management, there are really three separate and distinct dimensions: accumulation, distribution and legacy.

First, we earn and save it, then we live off it, and then we make sure it gets transferred to those we want to have it once we no longer need it.

Most people have no idea what is even possible with a well-created estate plan. There really are numerous design options, and people can control and protect their wealth from beyond the grave, so to speak, if they are so inclined.

The big thing for business owners to consider is that they really need to be mindful of maintaining congruency with their business and estate documents. The last thing you want to see is contradictory language with someone's buy-sell agreement and estate plan.

CHRIS. What is your approach to serving the financial needs of your clients?

MICHAEL. We take a team-based, holistic approach to financial planning and collaborate quite extensively with our client's other advisors. Our process is designed to assist with the full integration of personal, business, tax and estate planning. Taking this approach is optimal in terms of maximizing outcomes.

All too often, business owners have their financial affairs managed in a siloed format, by separate advisors who do not often communicate with one another. This can lead to missed opportunities across the entirety of one's financial landscape.

I often describe fully integrated planning like a classic Venn-diagram. There are three interlocking circles: personal planning, business planning, and tax and estate planning. The key element is the point of intersection. Successful planning requires understanding and then effectively managing the interrelationships between the seemingly disparate aspects of someone's financial life.

CHRIS. What are some of the vehicles used to protect a business owner's wealth from taxes?

MICHAEL. There are many vehicles and planning techniques that are highly effective when it comes to tax mitigation. Some of the more common options that come to mind would be company-sponsored retirement plans, IRAs, Roths, municipal bonds, and certain types of life insurance.

The real key when it comes to minimizing taxes is to remember that taxes are omnipresent, meaning they will probably affect you now and throughout the various stages of your life. In addition, they are subject to change. This means your tax planning needs to be fluid and ongoing.

Prudent tax planning should also be forward-thinking. Sometimes people make the mistake of making tax decisions solely based on the current tax year. This can subject folks to significant tax inefficiencies down the road.

CHRIS. What are the risks of not creating and executing a comprehensive financial plan?

MICHAEL. The primary risk is a missed opportunity. There are two types of people who benefit greatly from comprehensive financial planning.

Some folks truly need financial planning to save them from themselves and get them on track to financial independence.

Then there are the folks who don't necessarily need saving. They are doing well financially and have solid savings habits, earn healthy incomes, and do a decent job of managing debt. These people are often already financially independent, or very close to it. The benefit they receive from quality planning is the ability to maximize their financial potential by optimizing their overall efficiency and decision-making across all areas of their financial life.

Establish Family Governance

In addition to investing your wealth upon the sale of your business, family governance, as it relates to estate planning and protecting the wealth created for future generations, is critical. Family governance refers to the structures and processes used by families to clarify relationships, rights and responsibilities in making decisions based on a set of shared values in managing the family's business, wealth and future.

Any fool can make a fortune; it takes a man of brains to hold on to it after it's made.

—Cornelius "Commodore" Vanderbilt
to his son William Henry Vanderbilt

The Rothschilds and the Vanderbilts are a study in generational wealth and have experienced very different outcomes in the preservation of their legacy.

The Rothschilds initially acquired their fortune through international banking, then went on to invest in mining, energy, real estate, art, wine and many other sectors. Their wealth continued to grow through many generations, with their family motto being *Concordia, Integritas, Industria,* which translates to "Harmony, Integrity and Industry."

In comparison, the Vanderbilts amassed great wealth through the shipping and railroad industries. Until his death, Cornelius Vanderbilt, the family patriarch, was the richest man in America. By the third generation, however, the fortune stopped growing. The fourth generation continued to lead opulent lifestyles, and their billions of dollars of wealth was reduced to millions. In 1973, they had their first family reunion, and of the one hundred twenty members in attendance, there was not a single millionaire among them.

In contrast to the Rothschilds, the Vanderbilt family was fractured and had no strategy to maintain the wealth. The failure rate of family wealth preservation mirrors the rate of an unprepared family succession exit strategy.

It is estimated that 70 percent of wealthy families lose their wealth and family unity by the end of the second generation, and 90 percent lose it by the third generation.[22]

You don't have to be as rich as the Rothschilds or the Vanderbilts to fail. Lost wealth and family failure is an equal opportunity endeavor. To protect your wealth and family unit, it's critical to address family governance of the wealth you have created upon selling your business.

Prepare the Family for the Money

Tom and Cathy Rogerson of GenLeg Company, Inc., work with our clients to establish strong family governance and ensure their legacy (wealth and family health) will continue for generations to come.

They share the following insights on why family governance is critical and what you need to consider when strategizing to preserve the wealth you have worked so hard to achieve.

Most families fail through the generations at preserving wealth—both the tangible and intangible assets. Failure is defined as losing both the wealth and the family unity! The cause of this phenomenal erosion isn't bad investment management or poor tax planning. Rather, it's the lack of trust and communication around group decision-making.

Most modern estate planning doesn't address the critical issues of trust and communication within the family. In fact, many traditional estate plans increase the likelihood of wealth and family erosion.

In business, there is an adage that says "shirtsleeves to shirtsleeves in three generations." This refers to how the older generation starts with nothing and works hard to build their wealth. But by the time it's handed down to their great-grandchildren, there's nothing left. The key to changing this paradigm is family education and trust-building through an organized and prioritized family meeting process. Family meetings build trust, encourage interdependence, and help a family practice group decision-making. Governance practices need to be clear, relevant, followed and endowed.

In the last few years, with the dramatic increase in the federal estate tax exemption, many business owners that are below the exemption (or combined exemption for couples) have come to believe erroneously that they don't have an estate planning problem. This has led many people either to not update their plan or not plan at all. Setting aside the estate tax problems, they're missing the primary point and original purpose of estate planning.

Before there were federal estate taxes, there was estate planning. But it was about the people, the possessions, the process, the places, the history, the memories, and the family purpose—family legacy and harmony. It wasn't just about orderly and tax-efficient distribution, ongoing control, and protection of an estate. It was also focused on the purpose of the decedent, the purpose of the receivers (whether people or institutions), and the purpose of the family.

Over the last century, estate planners and families alike have become so focused on estate tax planning that the tax problem is all that advisors and parents seem to focus on. Some of the very techniques used to minimize taxes and protect assets from family conflict are making family governance and harmony more difficult for families to achieve.

A respected researcher once found that close to 80 percent of the wealth was gone within fifty years of the founder's death. That's not typically what the founders are hoping for, whether they keep the family business or sell it. So, we started looking at the research on why families were failing at preserving these businesses, their wealth and, more importantly, their families. It had almost nothing to do with all the tax planning they were doing, which blew me away. Instead, it had almost everything to do with the family dynamics and culture. It wasn't so much about whether they were preparing the money for the family—it was about whether they were preparing the family for the money.

You cannot plan your way out of this problem, and yet most people think planning is the solution.

Traditional estate planning strategies and tactics can actually be damaging to the family relationships and culture.

Here's a true example. Two brothers' parents died over ten years ago. One of the two brothers has four children; the other one has no children. One of the trusts that the parents set up is designed to provide financial resources for the future generations to pay for education, weddings, down payments on houses, and so on.

Which of these two brothers' families is benefiting most from that trust? The one with four kids. Which one hates that? The one with no kids. To get his "fair share" of the trust, he has sued his brother, the advisors that set up the trust, and the trustees that oversee the trust. He has sued three times now. He's lost all three times. Isn't that a great, wonderful story about the benefit of good planning? It just proves that planning is so powerful and good, right? The brothers now hate each other.

That was not the desired outcome of the parents. I knew the parents, and they'd be rolling over in their graves if they knew this was going to be the outcome.

What did they do wrong? They didn't prepare the next generation to understand the purpose of this trust. And they could've. It would've been so easy, but they didn't.

This example illustrates the approach I often see in traditional estate planning. Typical estate plans tend to do one of three things:

1. Confirm independence by dividing the assets independently for the children to do whatever they want. This is also known as "divide and conquer." I call that independence to the point of estrangement. It is also referred to as "hyper-individualism."

2. They try to force interdependence on the family by creating a foundation and giving everybody a board seat on the foundation. Or transferring the family vacation house to the children to share. Or transferring the business equally to the kids and saying, "Here are your shares, figure out your roles and how to work together." The intent is nice, but the implementation is too late and is forced on them. How successful is just putting these ideas in the will without preparing them along the way? Not very! And yet, it's amazing how many families and advisors continue to take this approach.

3. Or they just choose independent discretionary trustees to cut checks along the way, often creating entitlement, rather than discouraging it. I asked one parent if they were trying to raise children or adults, and of course they said adults. So, I asked them, "Why are you treating them like children for the rest of your life, and then having a trustee

treat them as children for the rest of their lives as well? Don't you think this might create the lack of motivation and entitlement that you said you were trying to avoid?"

Don't get me wrong. Protecting the wealth and enterprises is extremely important. It's just nowhere near as important as preparing the family to receive these blessings successfully and healthily.

At GenLeg, we have conducted surveys with over 450 families, and Williams and Preisser have researched over 3,500 families. Among all those surveys, the participating families admitted they are failing at preserving the connection between family members and have lost knowledge of their family's history within three generations.

In most cases, this disconnection of the family has sped up their loss of not only their intangible assets, but their tangible assets as well. By their own admission, these families failed at preserving both family unity and financial wealth—losing 60–70 percent of their wealth by the second generation and 80–90 percent by the third generation.

GenLeg and Williams and Preisser went one step further and asked participants, "You lived through the failure. From your perspective, having seen and lived through it, what went wrong?"

1. 60 percent said the reason for failure was due to lack of communication and trust around group decision-making in the family. That's the biggest issue by far.

2. 25 percent of the failures were due to unprepared heirs. It is only upon reflection that wealth creators recognize there's a difference between preparing

yourself for the wealth you create over time and preparing an heir for wealth they receive all at once from a gift, distribution or bequest. The wealth creator learned by necessity and probably had learned a lot before they even had the wealth. They most likely knew about budgeting, the need for saving, the effect of taxes, and so on. Yet the inheritor must learn how to effectively handle money voluntarily with no observed need. That requires an understanding of why it's important and a motivation to learn even though there is no need of the knowledge at the moment.

3. 10 percent of failure was due to no clarity of family purpose and no sense of a place or belonging within the family.

Add these up and it's 95 percent of the reason for the failure families were experiencing. The surveyed families attributed less than 5 percent of the failure to mistakes made in the planning and investing area.

These are cultural issues related to how the next generation was raised and prepared. With their financial success, the parents, often lovingly and intentionally, created the culture that caused this current disconnect, without foreseeing the problems that would arise.

A healthy family culture is necessary to preserve your wealth for future generations. One of the grandchildren of the Green family, of Hobby Lobby fame, told us, "Our family spends the time, money and energy at our family meetings to build the bridge of grace and trust so we can drive the truck of truth over it." Now that's a strong family culture!

Remember, the number one reason families pinpointed as the cause of their failure was "a lack of communication and trust around group decision-making."

Three entrepreneurship academics from Norway, Robert S. Nason, Thomas Markus Zellweger, and Mattias Nordqvist, researched and described a great cultural vision families should be encouraged to consider. They encouraged families to create an entrepreneurial culture that will persist for multiple generations.

What they were seeing is families that are succeeding multigenerationally had a familiness culture. And what they meant by that was not a fun social culture, but a true working knowledge of each other's strengths and abilities, along with strong trust, allowing transparent communication. This familiness culture was combined with an entrepreneurial culture to create a multigenerational enterprising family.

But always remember, a strong enterprise cannot hold a family together, but a strong family can hold an enterprise together.

The Green family succeeded because they had a strong family culture!

An executed wealth management strategy and a healthy family culture will ensure that your goals and intentions will be met, not only following the sale of the company but also after your death.

Creating a Master Exit Plan well in advance of the day you want to sell your business is vitally important to your post-ownership success. As a business owner, you are multifaceted, and your inevitable transition out of the business will impact every aspect of your life.

As you have discovered in this book, a successful exit requires more than just understanding how to sell a business. The first step in developing your MEP will identify and align your business, financial and personal goals so you are clear on what you want to achieve by exiting. The next step will include a valuation that will provide you with an understanding of whether your business is marketable and if the potential price could meet your financial goals.

If the answer is that your business isn't ready to go to market or can't fulfill your financial aspirations, an optimization plan will set you on the right road toward making the necessary changes, so when you do go to market in the future, you will be successful. The risk assessment step will ensure you and your business are properly protected and can quickly recover from any internal or external shocks. The next step will guide you in creating an exit strategy and selling your business. Once your company has sold and the wealth you have created is harvested, the final step of your plan will address the preservation of wealth.

A comprehensive Master Exit Plan will provide you with a roadmap that, when executed, will ensure that you can transition into the next chapter of your life with ease.

Be proactive, so you can successfully reach the finish line and protect your wealth, your family, and your legacy.

TAKE ACTION

- In preparation for closing your deal, meet with your wealth manager to create a wealth management strategy based on your risk tolerance and financial goals.

- Align yourself with a family governance professional who can work with you and your attorney in creating an estate plan that addresses your wealth and family health.

- Engage with an exit planning advisor today to begin the process of creating your Master Exit Plan.

Now go sell your business and live the life you desire. You deserve it!

Thank you for reading *Master Your Exit Plan.*
If you've enjoyed reading this book, please leave a review on
your favorite review site. It helps me reach more business
owners who may benefit from learning how to develop their
Master Exit Plan so they can successfully sell their business
when the time comes.

Acknowledgments

Having spent years traveling throughout the country speaking to business owners about their exit strategy and also engaging with entrepreneurial students in the Harvard class I lecture for, it was apparent they all carried a great deal of fear about exiting their businesses.

Selling a business is a complex process that impacts all aspects of an owner's existence, and the fear can be immobilizing.

When an owner doesn't prepare for their exit, they increase the risk that all their hard work will lead to a pitiful winding down of the business with no return for their investment of sweat equity.

This was my motivation as I put pen to paper.

My friend Jack Canfield once said to me, "You can't keep running all over the world educating one person at a time. You need to duplicate yourself and write a book!" Knowing he was right and with a pandemic that grounded me, I started this book to give owners the information they need to combat the fear.

It takes an army to pull off writing a book and there are many people to thank.

So, my first "thank you" goes to all of the entrepreneurs who shared their stories and fears with me throughout my travels. I learned a great deal from all of you.

Huge kudos to my case studies who bared all their fears, failures and successes to me. Matt whose story is so inspiring, Dawna the CEO who continues to impressively take the business she sold to new heights, Sam who overcame a tough first start at post-ownership, and John who sold the family business and created a lasting legacy with his philanthropic work.

Our clients at Legacy Partners deserve a huge shout-out as they unwittingly provided great material to help educate business owners and make the path just a little bit straighter for those walking behind them.

My contributors Jeff Carey, Michael Heberlein, and Tom and Cathy Rogerson who understood the gaps in knowledge our business owners needed and so eloquently shared their expertise. And Jonathan Kim who not only shared his expertise, but also put his Brown BA in English, MBA at Yale and Georgetown JD to great use suffering through the early drafts of this manuscript with my run-on sentences.

Jim Fitchett the instructor for Harvard University Extension's MGMT E-5420 Entrepreneurship and Innovation course that I have had the pleasure of guest lecturing for since 2014 afforded me a great platform to test run my material.

A thank you to my beta readers Brian Trzcinski, Sharon Saylor, and Ginger and Peter Wakem who shared their insight to ensure that the information was truly understandable and all loftiness removed!

Jaye Wahl, our lovely director of communications at Legacy Partners who squeezed in reading many drafts as she juggled her "real" work.

Then there are the many people who actually pieced this book together. Andrea Harley who provided a cover idea years before it was finished so I had my vision for the book.

The folks at Emerald Lake Books: Tara Alemany, who is absolutely the most detailed and patient publisher an author could ever dream of and who understood my humor and didn't strip it out of my book. Mark Gerber who designed the interior and painstakingly made the gold on the cover as dreamy as can be. Kudos to you both.

And many thanks to John Hart who has been an avid supporter of what we do at Legacy Partners and of this book.

Glossary of Terms

addbacks: Adjustments added back into the net profits of a company that will not be part of the company's future profit and loss statement, such as personal expenses, severance payments, or lawsuit settlements.

adjusted EBITDA: Expenses that are added to or subtracted from your EBITDA through the recasting process for all extraordinary, nonrecurring and discretionary expenses.

bolt on: A business that is purchased to add onto an existing company or platform.

book value: The net value of a business's assets found on its balance sheet.

business overhead insurance: Insurance that covers the fixed monthly overhead expenses required to keep a business running in the event the owner becomes disabled and cannot work.

buy-sell agreement: Also known as a "business will." This is a legal document that specifies how a partner's business shares will be distributed should a partner die or leave the business.

buy-side representative: An advisor who protects the interest of the buyer and guides them through the process of buying a business.

C corporation (or C-Corp): The standard (or default) corporate structure. Shareholders are taxed separately from the corporation.

capital gains tax: A tax on the profit from the sale of an asset.

clawback provision: A provision in a contract that forces the return of money to the company under specified circumstances.

confidential business profile (CBP): The first marketing document that is sent to your pool of buyers. It is a one-page, high-level overview (or "teaser") of a business, in which the company name is not disclosed.

confidential information memorandum (CIM): After a nondisclosure agreement is signed, this marketing document relays in-depth information about a business, including its projected financials, team and marketing plan. It is also sometimes known as the "offering memorandum."

cross-purchase buy-sell agreement: A contractual agreement that gives a company's partners or other shareholders the ability to purchase the shares of a partner upon their retirement or death.

data room: A virtual or physical location used to store documents, usually of a secure or privileged nature.

definitive purchase agreement (DPA): A contractual agreement outlining all the terms and conditions of a business sale.

discount rate: The interest rate used to determine the present value of future cash flows in a discounted cash flow analysis.

discretionary expenses: Personal expenses, such as meals and entertainment, travel and non-working family payroll, included in the financials for the sole purpose of minimizing a business owner's tax burden.

due diligence: The process of verifying all pertinent information about the seller's business.

earn-out: A payment that is contingent on meeting a specified metric typically tied to the income statement, such as sales or earnings. It could also be tied to a nonfinancial event, such as a regulatory approval or the retention of a big customer.

EBITDA (earnings before interest, taxes, depreciation and amortization): A measure of a company's overall financial performance.

efficiency ratio: The formula used to determine a company's ability to convert assets or leverage into revenue.

employee stock ownership plan (ESOP): A program that transfers the ownership of company stock to working employees.

enterprise value (EV): A reflection of the firm's value as a functioning entity, which is helpful in that it facilitates the comparison of companies with varying levels of debt.

entity purchase plan: A type of business succession plan for a company that has more than one owner. Each owner obtains a life insurance policy, and in the event of one owner's death, the remaining owner uses the life insurance to buy out the deceased owner's shares.

equity roll: A purchase of equity in the business made by the seller after the closing in lieu of receiving cash proceeds.

extraordinary expenses: Nonrecurring expenses, such as a severance package, a lawsuit settlement, a bad debt, or a loss on the sale of assets beyond what is normal and customary.

fair market value (FMV): Arm's-length value garnered in the open market based on the assumption that the buyer and seller are both fully informed and neither is under duress.

fair value (FV): An independently derived value used for financial reporting or legal purposes.

family governance: Rules or guidance used to govern the communication and business of a family enterprise.

fiat currency: A government-issued currency that is not backed by a physical commodity, such as gold or silver. Instead, its value is solely based on the government decree that issued it.

financial buyer: An investor, for example, a private equity group, that is looking for a return on their investment through cash flow and ultimately a future exit for their holding.

free cash flow (FCF): The cash available to pay dividends to investors and repay debts.

generally accepted accounting principles (GAAP): Accounting principles that are issued by the Financial Accounting Standards Board (FASB).

gross domestic product (GDP): The total value of all finished goods and services produced in a country within one year.

illiquid asset: An asset that cannot be easily or readily sold.

indication of interest (IOI): A nonbinding agreement issued in the form of a letter that communicates a buyer's interest in purchasing a business.

individual investor: An individual who buys a business with the intention of owning and running it.

initial public offering (IPO): Also known as a "stock launch." This is when a private company goes public through the sale of stock.

intangible assets: Nonphysical assets that have monetary value that drive revenue for a company, such as employees, customer relationships, patents and brands.

intrinsic value: Transferable value based on extensive quantitative and qualitative analysis.

investment value: The value of a business to a particular investor based upon their specific perception of the company.

IP documents: Legal documents stating the ownership of intellectual property.

key performance indicators (KPI): Quantifiable data that gauge your business's performance against a set of objectives or goals.

Lehman formula: A sliding scale used to determine the fee paid to a business brokerage firm, M&A firm, or investment bank.

letter of intent (LOI): A nonbinding document that outlines the chief terms of a specific deal.

leverage: Utilizing borrowed capital to fund a deal.

leveraged ESOP: An employee stock ownership plan that borrows capital based on the company's asset value to fund the plan.

lifestyle business: A business that centers on the lifestyle the owner is trying to achieve, and the income and flexibility needed to accomplish it.

liquidity ratio: The formula used to determine a business's ability to pay off short-term obligations. This is calculated as current assets minus current liabilities divided by current liabilities.

living trust: A legal entity that ensures that your assets, including the business, are kept out of probate and allows a confidential transfer of ownership.

loan covenant: A condition in a loan or bond issue that requires the borrower to fulfill certain conditions (for example, maintaining a certain debt-to-equity ratio).

management buyout (MBO): A sale structure in which the business's management team purchases the assets and operations of a company.

market approach: Also known as "comparable company analysis." A comparison of your business to the prices investors have paid for other similar companies.

market capitalization: The full market value of a company's outstanding shares.

market value (MV): The highest price received for an asset in the open market.

middle market: A company with annual revenue of $10 million to $1 billion.

multiple: A number used in a comparable company analysis that is set by the private capital markets to establish the relative value of a business by comparing a value to a relevant value driver.

negative interest rate policy: Sets interest rates below 0 percent to incentivize spending and lending.

net investment income tax (NIIT): Enacted in 2013, it is a tax that applies to income received from investment assets minus related expenses for individuals, estates and trusts whose income is above certain thresholds.

no-shop clause: A binding stipulation in the letter of intent that prevents the seller from engaging with another buyer.

noncompete agreement: A covenant to protect the buyer from a seller setting up another business and competing directly against the new ownership.

nondisclosure agreement: A contract by which one or more parties agree not to disclose confidential information they have shared with each other as a necessary part of doing business together.

nonqualified deferred compensation (NQDC): Compensation that has been earned but not received, so it is not yet subject to taxes.

pro forma financial statements: Financial reports based on hypothetical assumptions or projections.

profitability ratio: The ratio of a business's earnings to expenses.

qualitative analysis: Analysis of a company's value based on nonnumerical information, such as management expertise and client relationships.

quality of earnings (QOE): A report presented to a buyer after due diligence has been performed to substantiate the accuracy and sustainability of the company's historical earnings and future cash flow projections.

quantitative analysis: A type of financial analysis that uses mathematical and statistical modeling and research.

re-trading: A renegotiation of the terms of a deal, which is triggered by the discovery of potential risks or finalized information during due diligence.

recapitalization: An acquisition strategy where the seller retains some equity, and possibly a management position, in the company. This may include the ability to sell the remaining equity in the future for a second bite of the apple.

retained equity: A rollover of equity at the time of close, which may ultimately generate a second bite of the apple when the remaining interest is sold in the future.

return on investment (ROI): The profitability of an investment.

Sarbanes-Oxley Act of 2002 (SOX): A law the United States Congress passed on July 30, 2002, to help protect investors from fraudulent financial reporting by corporations.

S corporation (or S Corp): A small business corporation that is structured to pass income, deductions, losses and credit to shareholders for tax purposes.

Securities Exchange Commission (or SEC): A United States government agency that was formed on June 6, 1934, to regulate securities and protect investors.

secured notes: A secured debt owed by the buyer to the seller that is backed by a company's assets.

sell-side representative: An advisor who protects the interest of the seller and guides them through the process of selling a business.

SMART goals: An acronym that stands for Specific, Measurable, Achievable, Relevant and Time-bound. Following these criteria helps to create specific goals that are achievable within a certain time frame.

solvency ratio: A key metric calculated by net income plus depreciation divided by all liabilities. The result is used to measure an enterprise's ability to meet its long-term debt obligations.

step-up in basis: The adjustment of the cost basis of an asset to its current market value.

strategic buyer: A buyer who offers a synergistic fit to their existing operations, making the sum greater than the parts.

strategic value: The value placed on a business by a synergistic investor.

strengths, weaknesses, opportunities and threats (SWOT) analysis: An analytical tool used as an impartial assessment of where your business excels and what it lacks, plus growth opportunities to take advantage of and threats to mitigate.

tangible assets: Physical assets that have monetary value that drive revenue for a company, such as cash, inventory, property, plant and equipment.

Tax Cut & Jobs Act: Signed into law by President Trump in 2017, this act replaced the tiered corporate tax rate that ranged from 15 to 39 percent with a flat 21 percent and expanded first-year depreciation write-offs.

tax-free exchange: Private stock is exchanged for a public company stock. This is not really tax-free but tax-deferred. When the stock is sold in the future, the capital gains will be taxed.

trailing twelve months (TTM): The past twelve months of a company's performance data.

transferable value: The worth of a business to a buyer without the current owner in it.

trusteed cross-purchase agreement: An agreement in which a third party is used to act as a trustee or to carry out the requirements outlined in the agreement. This has tax benefits and requires fewer life insurance policies.

warranties, representations and indemnifications (WRI): A section of the definitive purchase agreement that warranties the accuracy and truth of a seller's representation statements.

weighted average cost of capital (WACC): A firm's cost of capital in which each category of capital is proportionately weighted, including stocks, bonds and long-term debt.

write-down: A type of re-trade, where the price is renegotiated because of finalized data verified during due diligence.

Notes

Introduction (page xxi)

1. *Business Owner Survey Report.* Business Enterprise Institute, Inc. 2019, accessed March 5, 2022, cdn.ymaws.com/www.aiccbox.org/resource/resmgr/docs/learn/2019_business_owner_survey.pdf.

Chapter 2: Which Exit Door Will You Choose? (pages 13–14)

2. *State of Owner Readiness Survey,* Exit Planning Institute, 2013, accessed March 5, 2022. exit-planning-institute.org/wp-content/uploads/2015/05/State_of_Owner_Readiness_2013_Report.pdf

3. PwC Data is sourced from research undertaken for the PwC Family Business Survey (2016), the PwC Next Gen Survey (2017), the PwC Family Business Survey (2018), Statistics Canada and PwC economic modeling. Once in a lifetime, PwC Canada, 2019, accessed March 5, 2022, pwc.com/ca/en/private-company-services/assets/pwc-canada-once-in-a-lifetime-report.pdf.

Chapter 3: What Happens Next in Your Life (pages 30, 37–38)

4. Exit Planning Institute, *Owner Readiness.*

5. Exit Planning Institute, *Owner Readiness.*

6. "The health benefits of strong relationships," Harvard Health Publishing, accessed March 5, 2022, health.harvard.edu/staying-healthy/the-health-benefits-of-strong-relationships.

Chapter 4: How Much Money Do You Need? (pages 43, 46)

7. Exit Planning Institute, *Owner Readiness*.

8. "How to prepare for rising health care costs," Fidelity, accessed March 5, 2022, fidelity.com/viewpoints/personal-finance/plan-for-rising-health-care-costs.

Chapter 5: Who Can You Count On? (page 59)

9. "2019 Small Business Finance and HR Report," OnPay, accessed March 5, 2022, onpay.com/hr/basics/2019-small-business-finance-hr.

Chapter 6: Will Your Business Attract a Buyer? (page 77)

10. *Market Pulse*, International Business Brokers Association, 2019, accessed March 5, 2022, assets.ibba.org/wp-content/uploads/2020/02/2019-ibba-q1.pdf.

Chapter 7: What's Your Business Worth? (page 98)

11. DealStats (formerly Pratt's Stats) by Business Valuation Services serves as a great resource for statistics.

Chapter 8: How Risky is Your Business? (pages 106, 117)

12. Exit Planning Institute, *Owner Readiness*.

13. *Retaining Talent*, SHRM Foundation, 2008, accessed March 5, 2022, blog.shrm.org/sites/default/files/reports/Retaining%20Talent-%20A%20Guide%20%28Q1%29.pdf.

Chapter 9: Do You Sell or Do You Grow? (pages 123, 125)

14. "Small biz owners ignoring succession advice: Poll," CNBC, accessed March 5, 2022, cnbc.com/2015/04/13/ew-small-biz-have-an-exit-plan.html.

15. Average selling price in 2020 per Pitchbook.

16. Net investment income tax.

Chapter 10: What's Your Timing? (pages 137–138)

17. "Federal Debt: Total Public Debt as percent of Gross Domestic Product," FRED Data, accessed March 5, 2022, fred.stlouisfed.org/series/GFDEGDQ188S.

18. "National debt in the United States in relation to gross domestic product (GDP) from 2016 to 2021, with a forecast to 2026," Statistica, accessed March 5, 2022, statista.com/statistics/269960/national-debt-in-the-us-in-relation-to-gross-domestic-product-gdp/.

19. "US National Debt by Year," The Balance, accessed March 5, 2022, thebalance.com/national-debt-by-year-compared-to-gdp-and-major-events-3306287.

20. "Just How Many Baby Boomers Are There," Population Reference Bureau, accessed March 5, 2022, prb.org/resources/just-how-many-baby-boomers-are-there.

Chapter 14: Will Due Diligence Kill You? (page 178)

21. A due diligence checklist often guides the process, permitting a buyer to see what obligations, liabilities, problematic contracts, intellectual property issues, and litigation risks they're assuming. You can find a sample checklist on the Upcounsel website at upcounsel.com/due-diligence-checklist.

Chapter 15: Crossing the Finish Line (page 197)

22. "70% of Rich Families Lose Their Wealth by the Second Generation," Time, accessed March 5, 2022, time.com/3925308/rich-families-lose-wealth/.

Index

A

accountants. *See* CPAs
acqui-hiring, 81
acquisition strategy, 32, 90
addbacks, 95–96
adjusted EBITDA, 94, 98
adjustments
  to EBITDA, 95–96, 179, 182
    See also adjusted EBITDA
  post-closing, 182
advisory fees, 57, 59
amortization, 94
asset
  allocation, 65–66, 171, 193
  approach, 93, 99
  assignability, 169
  distribution, 16, 61–63, 200
  protection, 198
  sale, 66, 94, 168–71, 174
  structure, 169–70, 172
assets
  personal. *See* personal assets
  step-up in basis of, 169–70
  taxes on, 169, 171

attorney
  for document review, 64, 69
  estate planning, 61–63
  M&A, 49, 63–64, 68–71, 175
  transactional, 53, 63, 167
auctions, 26, 151–52
  limited, 146, 151, 167, 180

B

baby boomers, 21, 138
benchmarks, 100, 132, 173–74
book value, 56, 92, 99
business brokers, 50–54, 56, 151
businesses
  family. *See* family business
  middle-market, 9, 84, 132,
    139, 172
business goals, 8–10, 13, 27, 41,
    44, 70
business owners
  buy-sell agreements and, 108–9
  common mistakes of, 146
  financial planning and, 192–94
  insurance coverage for, 116–17
business plan, 61, 194

business valuation, 43–44,
90–92, 127
process, 99
types of, 93
business value, 42–43, 60, 84,
87, 90–92
book value, 99
calculation of, 167
confidentiality and, 186
as a criteria for selling, 132
discount rate and, 77–78
due diligence and, 66
economic impact on, 137
effect of decisions on, 89–90
effect of normalization process
on, 96
in financial plans, 44
five Big D's and, 107
goodwill and, 168
growth, 140
human capital and, 81
KPIs related to, 100
optimization of, 46, 54, 123
pandemic appreciation on, 139
post-closing adjustments, 182
premature disclosure and, 157
protection of, 107, 116
risk and, 140
rule of thumb, 99
sales process and, 82
buyer pool, 143, 146, 149, 152, 155
buyers
external, 26
types of, 146–51
buy-sell agreements, 107–16
benefits of, 108
funding of, 112
mechanics of, 109–11

for single-owner busi-
nesses, 108–9
structure of, 111–12
tax considerations, 114
triggering events, 107–12, 115
with uninsurable part-
ners, 112–14
buy-side representation,
52, 57–58

C
capital gains, 41, 119, 169–74
federal tax, 134–35
Carey, Jeffrey, 107–18, 181
cash, 97, 134–35, 140, 169,
172–73, 182
cash flow, 146, 192
free, 93, 96–97, 149
future, 90, 96–98
predictable, 9, 25, 98
CBP. See confidential business profile
CCA. See comparable
company analysis
C corporation, 20, 169–70
certified public accountant,
59–60, 71, 179
children, asset distribution
among, 16–17, 62, 109, 199–201
CIM. See confidential information memorandum
closing
costs, 71–72
delays, 64, 70–71, 179
process, 70
company stock, 20, 171–73
comparable company analysis,
93, 98

confidence, 134, 137–40
confidential business
    profile, 155–56
confidential information memo-
    randum, 156, 159–60
confidentiality, 151–52, 157–58
contingency plans, 79, 87, 105–6
continuity plan, 105–7, 116, 119
corporate culture, 82, 117, 164–65
costs
    of capital, 135
    closing, 71–72, 171
    of credit, 139
    of indemnification obliga-
        tions, 67
    of insurance coverage, 181
    of personal goals, 44–45
    of post-ownership life, 46
CPAs, 56, 59–60, 71, 171–72,
        175, 179
    poor advice from, 56
    tax analysis from, 125
    transactional, 49, 56, 171
    as trusted advisors, 59
credit, 134–37, 139–40, 172
cross-purchase agree-
        ments, 111–12
    trusteed, 111

D
data room, 69, 177–78
DCF. *See* discounted cash flow
deal structure, 168–71, 174
deal team, 49–50, 55–56,
        143, 145–46, 164, 167–68,
        170–71, 175
deal terms, 65, 68, 132, 184
debt, 21, 95, 148, 182

deferred compensation plan, 118
definitive purchase agreements,
        63–70, 170, 175, 180, 182
    key terms, 180
depreciation, 94, 172
discounted cash flow, 93, 97–98
discount rate, 77, 88, 97–98
DPA. *See* definitive
        purchase agreements
due diligence, 15, 33, 65–66, 68,
        70, 177–81
    checklist, 159, 211–223
    prolonged, 96
Dutch Tulip Mania, 137

E
earnings, 94, 139, 147
earn-out, 65, 132, 173–74, 184
EBITDA, 7, 50, 52–53, 86, 88, 94,
        167, 179
    adjusted, 94–96
    See also adjusted EBITDA
efficiency ratios, 100
employees, 184–86
    hiring away, 157
    sale to, 22
employee stock ownership plans,
        20–22, 52
    cons, 21
    failure, 21–22
    pros, 20
employment agreements,
        174–75, 184
engagement agreements, 145
enterprise value, 92, 105, 148
equity position, 22–23, 132, 147,
        162, 172

ESOP. *See* employee stock owner-
    ship plans
estate planners, 49, 198
estate planning, 43, 54, 61–63,
    194, 197–201
    buy-sell agreement and, 110
    effect on financial plan-
        ning, 193–94
    family governance and,
        196–98, 200
estate taxes, 198
EV. *See* enterprise value
exclusivity, 67, 145, 164, 175
exit goals, 9, 11, 53
exit planning advisor, 52–54,
    56–57, 72, 167, 171, 175
exit readiness, 126-128, 130
exit strategy, 9, 49, 56, 60,
    120, 132
    ESOP or MBO, 20–22
    family succession, 14–18
    for financial investor, 23
    IPO, 18–20
    liquidation, 24–26
    recapitalization, 22–23
    third-party sale, 26–27, 81
    types of, 14
expenses
    discretionary, 94–95
    extraordinary, 60, 94
    personal, 94

F
fair market value, 92
fair value, 92
familiness culture, 203

family
    business, 17, 109, 129
    discount, 15, 32, 44
    failure, 197, 201–3
    goals, 109
    governance, 49, 196–203
    office group, 22
    relationships, 38, 199
family successions, 14–18, 44,
    52, 129
    cons, 15
    failure of, 15–17, 44, 197, 203
    pros, 14
FCF. *See* free cash flow
fiat currency, 136
finance team, 79, 86
financial
    advisors, 51, 192
    analysis, 42
    buyers, 51–52, 98, 130, 132,
        146–47, 149, 162
    goals, 8, 10, 29–30, 43–44, 55,
        91–92, 123, 192
        80-percent rule, 42
    investor, 22–23, 134
    normalization of statements,
        53, 93–94, 96
    planning, 41–44, 47, 54, 56, 91,
        105, 192–95
    pro forma statements, 96
five Big D's, 107
free cash flow, 77, 93, 96–97, 149
FV. *See* fair value

G
goodwill, 168–69, 172, 174
Greens, 202–3

H
happiness, 11, 34–35, 38
health care, 45
  proxy. *See* power of attorney
health insurance, 117
Heberlein, Michael, 192–95
human capital, 79–81, 117,
   150, 162

I
identity loss, 31, 33
income
  approach, 93
  replacement, 42, 46, 192
  sources, 42, 44
indemnification obliga-
   tions, 65–67
indemnifications, 170, 181
indication of interest, 160, 180
individual investors, 50, 150–51
inflation, 135–36, 140
initial public offering, 14, 18–20
  cons, 19
  pros, 19
insurance, 49, 62, 110–17, 181
  business, 106–7, 116
  to fund buy-sell agreements,
   110–12, 114
  life, 62, 112–13, 115, 117, 195
  professionals, 49
  WRI, 181–82
intangible assets, 5, 24, 56, 90,
   120, 156
  business drivers and, 88
  business owner as, 162
  human capital as, 81, 117,
   158, 165
  preservation of, 197, 201

value of, 5
intellectual property, 69, 87–88
interest, 94, 136
interest rates, 133, 135–37, 140
  negative, 136
Internal Revenue Service, 15, 21,
   59–60, 66, 96, 171
investment
  bankers, 50–52, 54, 56
  banks, types of, 51
  strategy, 60–61, 191
    See also wealth management
  value, 92
investors, 80–82, 84–85, 96–97,
   132, 134, 137, 156, 159
  active, 152
  cash availability and, 134
  customer diversification
   and, 84
  EBITDA and, 88, 94
  human capital and, 80–81
  legal issues and, 87
  motivation of, 139
  operations analysis and, 85
  perceived risk and, 85
  price and, 98
  profitability and, 94
  retail, 85
  revenue sustainability and, 82
  risk and, 88
  role in M&A cycle, 137
  sale price and, 88
  types of, 146–51
  value proposition and, 80
  See also financial investors;
   individual investors; strategic buyers
IOI. *See* indication of interest

IPO. *See* initial public offering

IRS. *See* Internal Revenue Service

K

key contracts, 65–66

key employees, 13, 81–82, 87, 107, 117, 158, 161

  buy-sell agreements and, 62

  deferred compensation plan, 118–20

Kim, Jonathan, 64–72

L

legal team, 79, 86

Lehman Formula, 145

letter of intent, 59–60, 63–69, 160, 163–64, 175, 180

  binding provisions, 67–69

  nonbinding provisions, 65–66

leverage, 148–49, 178

Levi Strauss & Co., 17–18

liabilities, 63, 65, 169–70, 181

life insurance. *See* insurance, life

lifestyle business, 24, 50, 53

liquidation, 14, 24–25, 99

  cons, 24

  pros, 24

liquidity

  events, 8, 22, 30, 44, 49, 54

  options, 13

  ratios, 100

  second event, 149

living expenses, 45

living trusts, 61

LOI. *See* letter of intent

M

M&A advisors, 49–54, 56–57, 69, 71, 92, 158, 171

M&A cycles, 20–21, 26, 133, 137–38, 140

management buyout, 14, 20–21, 52

  cons, 21

  pros, 20

management team, 20–21, 79–81, 156, 160–61, 163–64, 185

  contingency planning, 81

  depth of, 80–82

  succession plan, 81

market

  approach, 93, 98

  conditions, 46–47, 124, 132

  timing, 26–27, 131

  value, 25, 43–44

    fair. *See* fair market value

marketing

  documents, 155–56, 159

  plans, 79, 84–85

Master Exit Plan, 4, 9, 13, 29, 89, 123, 204

M&A team, 49, 60, 145, 167, 182. *See also* deal team

MBO. *See* management buyout

MEP. *See* Master Exit Plan

N

NDA. *See* nondisclosure agreements

negotiations, 64, 68, 167–75

nonbinding agreements. *See* letter of intent

noncompete agreements, 27, 67, 174

nondisclosure agreements, 67, 69, 146, 156–58
nonqualified deferred compensation plans, 117–20
  employee advantages, 120
  employer advantages, 119–20
  funding, 119
  structure of, 118–19
normalization. *See* process, normalization
NQDC. *See* nonqualified deferred compensation plan

O

operations, 60, 79–81, 85, 94, 106, 149–50
  and contingency planning, 87
  insurance for, 116
opportunity cost, 124–25
optimization strategies, 56
ordinary income tax, 135, 169, 171, 173–75

P

partial sales, 22–23
partners, 33, 107–8, 112–15
  death of, 107, 115
  uninsurable, 112–14
payments, 151
  earn-out, 173
  family succession, 16
  taxes on, 174
  types of, 172–73
PEG. *See* private equity group
personal
  assets, 43
  expenses, 46

goals, 10, 29–30, 34–39, 41
  See also costs, of personal goals
post-ownership
  financial needs, 44–46
  goals, 39, 44, 46
  life, costs of, 41
  plan, 29, 34, 37, 41–42
  regrets, 30–32, 34–35, 37, 42
  social life, 37
post-ownership drivers
  intellectual, 36
  physical, 37
  social, 37
power of attorney, 62
price, 21, 58, 65, 84, 96, 152, 168, 170
  adjustments to, 179
  as component of DPA, 68
  earn-outs and, 173
  family discounts and, 44
  fees and, 145
  M&A cycle and, 133
  market approach and, 98
  negotiation of, 167
  as provision of LOI, 65
  recurring revenue and, 83
  renegotiation, 182
  risk and, 78, 162
  stock as currency for, 134
private equity groups, 22, 52, 56, 147, 149
  case study, 157
  types of, 149
private investment group, 22

process
  closing, 70
  normalization, 53, 93
  recasting, 94
profitability, 96
  ratios, 100
provisions
  binding, 67
  buyer protection, 146
  indemnification, 66
  nonbinding, 65–66

Q

qualitative analysis, 77, 79, 155
quantitative analysis, 93,
    99–100, 155

R

readiness, 125, 133
  See also exit readiness
recapitalizations, 14, 22–23,
    147–48, 172
  cons, 23
  pros, 22
recasting, 94–95
regrets
  See post-ownership, regrets
  See seller's remorse
relationships
  with accountant, 59
  effect on health, 38
  family, 38, 196, 199
  with wealth manager, 61
representations, 67, 170, 181
residual value, 97
re-trading, 179–80
return on investment, 25–26, 82,
    117, 124, 145–46, 155, 159
revenue growth, 82

risk, 24, 30, 148, 170
  business, 162
  of business ownership, 26,
      124–25, 186
  confidentiality, 58, 152, 186
  earn-out, 173
  industry, 161–62
  industry disruption as, 139
  management, 105
  private equity groups and, 149
  recapitalzation, 148
  reduction of, 26, 87–88, 105–6,
      123, 149, 169, 172
  tolerance, 60, 192
Rogerson, Tom and
    Cathy, 197–203
Rothschilds, 196–97

S

sale proceeds, 193
sales process, 79, 82–84
Schwinn, 15
S corporation, 169–70
seller meeting prepara-
    tion, 160–63
seller's remorse, 30–31
sell-side representation, 52, 57
shares, 21, 91, 109, 111
SMART goals, 38
social life, 31, 37–38
solvency ratios, 100
spouse, 107, 115–16
step-up in basis, 114, 169–70
stock sale, 66, 168–71, 174, 178
strategic
  buyers, 21, 32, 51–52, 57, 149–50
  plan, 79–80, 89
  value, 92
structure. *See* deal structure

success fee, 51, 145
SWOT analyses, 77

T
tangible assets, 90, 99, 201
taxes, 56, 94, 109, 111–12, 169,
    193–95, 198
  deferred, 171–72
  mitigating, 54, 56, 171, 175, 195
terms, 65, 67, 151, 164, 171,
    173, 184
third-party buyer, 146
third-party sale, 14, 22, 26–27, 44,
    52, 81
  cons, 26
  pros, 26
three Big C's for investors, 134
transferable value, 4, 27, 43,
    78–79, 88–90, 123, 131,
    133, 139
transition plan, 18

V
valuation, 43–44, 56, 91–93, 96,
    110, 123, 149, 179
  process, 93, 95–96, 133
value
  drivers, 79, 97
  gaps, 56, 77, 93
  proposition, 80
  residual, 93, 97–98
Vanderbilts, 196–97
virtual data room. *See* data room

W
warranties, 67, 170, 181
  representations and indemnifi-
    cations insurance. *See* insur-
    ance, WRI
wealth, 10–11, 43, 109, 124,
    191–92, 194–99
  family preparation, 202
  harvesting, 89
  managers, 49, 60
  protection of, 49, 195, 201
wealth management, 107,
    191–95, 203
will, 62. *See also* estate planning
winner's curse, 80
working capital, 82, 95, 181–82
WRI. *See* insurance, WRI
write-downs, 179

Z
Zildjian, 17

About the Contributors

Jeff Carey

Jeff Carey is a Senior Partner and Managing Director at Vertex Planning Group, part of the Commonwealth Financial Group, providing a single-source, comprehensive wealth management solution for his clients. He specializes in the full integration of personal, business and estate planning, as well as tax mitigation strategies.

Jeff reviews all aspects of his clients' financial lives—including their goals, objectives, desired timeline, and risk tolerance. He and his team then integrate these aspects to develop a comprehensive strategy tailored to each individual client. His personalized process allows clients to pursue their goals with purpose, clarity and a long-term view.

Jeff graduated from the University of Massachusetts Dartmouth with a BS in Business Management and International Marketing. He maintains a Certified Family Business Specialist (CFBS®) designation. In addition, he holds a Life, Accident and Health license, as well as Series 7 and 66 securities registrations.

Jeff currently lives in Swansea, Massachusetts, with his wife, Judy, and daughter, Ava.

Michael Heberlein

Michael Heberlein is a partner at Commonwealth Financial Group. His primary focus is assisting clients in achieving their goals by integrating all facets of their financial lives—including retirement planning, investment strategies, risk management, estate planning, and tax mitigation.

It is his goal to understand the dreams, desires and intricacies of every client's financial and personal lives while educating clients on the vast portfolio of financial planning concepts, strategies and tools applicable to their unique situation. He measures success by the client's understanding of a strategy's potential impact and the confidence with which the client can implement the plan. Michael has also dedicated a portion of his practice to working with families who have a loved one with a special need.

Michael graduated magna cum laude from the University of Massachusetts-Amherst with a dual degree in Finance & Operations Management and Sport Management. In addition, he holds a Life, Accident and Health license, as well as Series 7, 6, 63 and 65 securities registrations.

He lives in Medford, Massachusetts, with his wife, Chelsea.

Jonathan B. Kim

Jonathan Kim assists Legacy Partners' clients as lead counsel on M&A and related strategic transactions through his legal practice, Jonathan B. Kim, PA. He has over thirty years of asset, legal and executive management experience developed in the United States and abroad.

He obtained his bachelor's degree from Brown University, his MBA from Yale University, and his JD from Georgetown University, and studied at the European University Institute in Florence, Italy.

He is a member of the state and federal bars of Connecticut, the District of Columbia, Florida, Georgia, Massachusetts, New York and the Southern and Eastern Districts of New York. Jonathan holds FINRA Series 7, 24 and 63 registrations as well as real estate licenses in Florida and New York, and annuity, life and health insurance licenses in Florida.

Jonathan lives in Coral Gables, Florida, with his wife, Gabrielle, and their Pomeranian, Gatsby.

Tom and Cathy Rogerson

Tom Rogerson, cofounder of GenLeg Company, Inc., is a recognized leader and pioneer in family governance and legacy planning. He holds a BA in Economics from Ithaca College. After four decades of introducing, creating and delivering family legacy services at State Street Global Advisors, BNY Mellon, and Wilmington Trust, Tom teamed up with his wife, Cathy, a certified relationship coach to start GenLeg.

Tom and Cathy have worked with over 270 families, facilitating their meetings and creating a shared legacy vision and plan, transparent family trust and communication, a combined familiness culture and entrepreneurial mindset, a philanthropic vision, and a next-generation development plan. They then collaborate with a client's advisor team to endow the family meeting process as part of the estate plan, allowing the process to last generationally.

Cathy graduated with a BA in Social Work from Ohio Wesleyan University. She holds certifications in marriage coaching, life coaching, emotionally focused therapy, solution-focused therapy, and pre-marriage coaching from the American Association of Christian Counselors and Prepare/Enrich.

About the Author

CHRIS VANDERZYDEN, CPA, CVGA, CEPA, is a founding partner of Legacy Partners, LLLP, an exit planning and M&A advisory firm dedicated to serving privately held, middle-market business owners by creating and executing successful exit strategies resulting in the harvesting and preservation of wealth.

She began her career as a CPA for Coopers & Lybrand, the company that later became PricewaterhouseCoopers following a merger, and subsequently served as an asset manager with Northwest Asset Management in Los Angeles.

Following her positions in the corporate world, Chris became an entrepreneur and has successfully sold multiple businesses. She has over twenty years of experience consulting for privately held businesses as they grow and ultimately execute their exit plans.

Chris speaks internationally on exit planning and mergers and acquisitions, is an expert contributor for media outlets, and is a guest lecturer for Harvard University Extension's Entrepreneurship and Innovation course.

She is also the best-selling author of *7 Steps to Entrepreneurial Victory*.

If you're interested in having Chris speak to your group, association or organization, either online or in person, you can contact her at emeraldlakebooks.com/vanderzyden.

About Legacy Partners

LEGACY PARTNERS, LLLP, is an exit planning advisory firm that specializes in mergers and acquisitions that is dedicated to serving privately held business owners in the middle market.

The firm is comprised of best-in-class expert advisors who utilize a comprehensive approach that aligns an owner's business, personal and financial objectives with their Master Exit Plan. The execution of the plan to sell the business is then guided by our mergers and acquisitions team, who offers sell-side-only representation that results in the harvesting of wealth.

For more information, visit legacypartnersllp.com.

For more great books, please visit us at
emeraldlakebooks.com.

EMERALD LAKE
BOOKS
Sherman, Connecticut

Printed in Great Britain
by Amazon